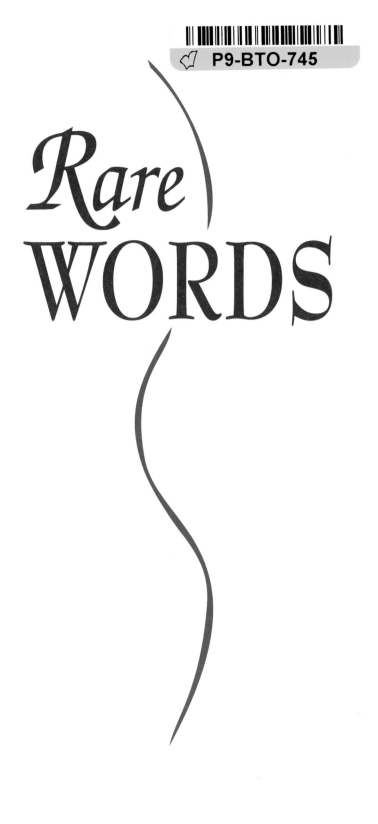

Rare
WORDS

Rare
WORDS

and
ways to master
their meanings

500 ARCANE BUT
USEFUL WORDS FOR
LANGUAGE LOVERS

Jan Leighton   **Hallie Leighton**

LEVENGER
PRESS
Delray Beach, Florida

Published by
Levenger Press
420 South Congress Avenue
Delray Beach, Florida 33445-4696
www.LevengerPress.com

The excerpt from George Orwell's "Politics and the English
Language" is from his volume SHOOTING AN ELEPHANT AND OTHER
ESSAYS, copyright 1946 by Sonia Brownell Orwell and renewed 1974
by Sonia Orwell. Reprinted by permission of Harcourt, Inc.

The epigraph by David Crystal is from *The Cambridge Encyclopedia
of the English Language.* Copyright © Cambridge University Press
1995. Reprinted with the permission of Cambridge University Press.

Library of Congress Cataloging-in-Publication Data

Leighton, Jan, 1921-
  Rare words and ways to master their meanings : 500 arcane but
useful words for language lovers / Jan Leighton, Hallie Leighton.
     p. cm.
Includes bibliographical references and index.
  ISBN 1-929154-12-7 (trade paper)
 1. Vocabulary. I. Leighton, Hallie, 1970- II. Title.
  PE1449 .L366 2003
  428.1--dc21

                                          2002015769

Cover and book design by Levenger Studios
Illustrations by Lee Passarella

In loving memory of
the two Roses.

Vocabulary is the Everest of a language.

> – David Crystal, author of
> *The Cambridge Encyclopedia
> of the English Language*

Contents

Publisher's Note

"What is the use of a book...without pictures or conversations?" asked Alice of *Wonderland* fame. And what is the use of language without picturesque words that enliven conversations?

I confess: I knew only a handful of these rare words when Jan Leighton and his daughter, Hallie, sent us their manuscript. Faced with words like **sumpsimus** and **consuetude**, my vocabulary rated only a medium rare. *Rare Words* was as if Alice had unlocked another door in her Wonderland to a language that we all spoke but had yet to discover.

The Leightons are adept at putting us at ease with words we've just met. With some, it's the concise definition; with many, the interesting etymology; and for others, it's the clever mnemonics they've devised that create an instant picture in our minds, as **manqué** and **antaean** did in mine.

I intend to use my rare words—not all the time, but the way a chef might use a pungent spice. Now that I know another way to express happiness (**eudemonia**), strong (**roborean**) and crested (**pileated**), I'm eager to add more color to my conversation. Uncommon words, when they are just the right words, help keep our language vibrant and make our descriptions precise.

A friend once told me that he takes pleasure in collecting antiques because it connects him to others of a similar passion. It is the same for those of us who collect words: our love of language connects us. Here for your collection, to use and enjoy, are 500 rare, colorful and splendid words.

– Steven Leveen

Authors' Proems

Rare Words is for language lovers who are tired of seeing the same easy-to-intermediate words and who are hungering for real toughies. To paraphrase Bessie Smith (and Mae West, and Flannery O'Connor), a good, challenging word nowadays is hard to find.

Rare Words is a repository of such finds: **oneiric**, **Tempean**, **patulous** and others of like strangeness. Most of the words are so uncommon that you may wonder whether we have made them up. They are all authentic. Though some have just recently made their way over from other languages (such as **anlage** from German), and a handful are considered archaic or obsolete (**whilom** and **yclept**), each one can be found in at least one English-language dictionary. Not one dictionary, however, contains all 500 of these words—not even the *Oxford English Dictionary*.

You might wonder how words that are so little known can be useful. If the purpose of language is to make oneself understood, what is the point of dropping a word like **indaba** into one's writing or conversation?

Don't underestimate the pliancy of the English language. Today's rarity is tomorrow's favorite word. A generation ago, Richard Burton christened his yacht *ChaLizma* in honor of his wife Elizabeth Taylor. The pun was lost on most; *charisma* was then an obscure word. The word has since gained in currency what it has lost in charisma.

As recently as three years ago, a mischievous new German transplant meaning "delight in a friend's misfortune" was unknown and unpronounceable to most English speakers. *Schadenfreude* may still be unpronounceable (shah-den-FROY-duh), but today it is less of a novelty word among English speakers, and in certain circles, a staple.

Authors' Proems

Other rare words are coming into currency as we write this. This book itself may bring many of these words into circulation, thanks to devoted wordaholics like you.

Even when we use words that remain rare, our use of these words will not be forgotten; in fact, the words may help people remember you. Like Proust's tea-soaked madeleine, a rare word has the power to trigger decades-old memories. Recently, I ran across *ligula* while looking up another word. I was suddenly transported to a kitchen in upper Manhattan and my childhood, hearing my father say "Where's the *ligula*?" while looking for a funnel. Saying the word out loud, I can picture the striated wood panels on the walls of our kitchen, the icebox in the corner and even my mother's perfectly stuffed green peppers on the table. I can still see and hear my father's frustration as he searches for both the funnel and the plain English word to describe it, *ligula* being his second choice.

It is a mystery how my father, born and raised in East Harlem, with no knowledge of other languages save a smattering of Polish, was able to come up with an obscure Latin word but not a common English one. But if he once unwillingly summoned the word, the word now has the power to summon *him*, something no everyday word could do. It is remarkable how we remember people for the words they use, especially the rarities. In the end, words define *us* just as much as we define them.

– Jan Leighton

I share my dad's fondness for words, especially ones I've never heard before. But I hesitated when he asked me to join him on this project. I was haunted by the ghost of George Orwell—specifically, this passage from his essay "Politics and the English Language":

> Bad writers, and especially scientific,
> political, and sociological writers, are nearly
> always haunted by the notion that Latin or

Authors' Proems

> Greek words are grander than Saxon ones,
> and unnecessary words like expedite,
> ameliorate, predict, extraneous, deracinated,
> clandestine, subaqueous, and hundreds of
> others constantly gain ground from their
> Anglo-Saxon numbers.

I worried that in the wrong hands, such a book could wreak havoc on the English language. There was always the danger that it could contribute to **fastuous**, **fustian preciosity** (showy, pretentious, excessive elegance of literary style). This book had the potential to equip people who use language as a means to distance themselves from others rather than communicate with them. Perhaps, then, this book should be banned. Why teach perfectly decent writers the word **execrable** when its Saxon synonym, *loathsome*, will serve them just fine and make them more universally understood? Are we abetting bad writing?

I had a dark night of the soul, but then I realized: George Orwell was wrong. At least on that point. Although many words have synonyms, some of which are more familiar, no word possesses an exact clone. A synonym is just that: a word with similar—not identical— meaning. There is always a tiny shade of difference in meaning that makes one word the most appropriate in a specific context. Even the varying sounds of words contribute to a word's DNA: the very sound of **execrable** lends it a nuance that is slightly more execrable than *loathsome* is. Finding the exact word for the occasion is what makes writing challenging and rewarding.

As you peruse this book, you may ask when it is appropriate to start using these words. My advice is: not right away. I treat words I have just learned like new acquaintances; no matter how well we hit it off on a first meeting, I don't assume intimacy. Just as I would not pretend to be a close friend of someone I'd just met, I would not drop words I had just learned into a conversation. I might feel a little more familiar with

Authors' Proems

a person after running into him or her at a couple of parties; likewise, I would wait to see or hear my newly acquired word used a couple times before using it myself. And you would be surprised how soon you are likely to run into a word you have just met. Once your antenna is attuned, your rare word magically starts showing up, even though you'd swear you'd never heard it before.

This language of ours could stand freshening up. A number of words have become stale from overuse. *Awesome* may have once been an awesome word, but today it is unlikely to inspire anything, let alone awe. *Rock* is dead—not the music genre, but the verb (as in "That show rocked!"). It died from excessive use. There are far more interesting words out there. May we introduce you?

– Hallie Leighton

Proem is a rare word for preface.

How to Use this Book
(and Remember Rare Words)

This is a browser's book. We call it an undictionary because the entries are nonalphabetical and random, the way one encounters rare words in real life. (We also find that reading too many difficult words alphabetically can be a bit numbing.) You will, however, find two more traditional avenues for locating a word. An alphabetical listing by categories (e.g., *Plants and Animals*, *Learning and Knowledge*) is in the front of the book. An index of the words is in the back.

Rare words and remembrance

The words are grouped into 365 entries so that you can, if you wish, master just a single entry a day. Within nearly every entry is a device to help make the word or words memorable. For some, an example or anecdote makes the word more manageable. For others, it's the contrast of two words that are similar in spelling but different in meaning, or the coupling of two or more words of similar meanings.

Sometimes a rare word is paired with a medium rare one of related meaning or origin, as **pruritic** is with **prurient**, to help in memorizing both. Often the etymology helps to recall meaning.

And many times, mastery is through mnemonics. You'll see these links presented in this format (as this one for **urticate**):

❖ To urticate is to h**urt** by stinging.

These puns and other wordplays serve as memory joggers, helping to link the sound of a word to its meaning—the way h**urt** links urticate to its meaning of sting.

Unlocking the meaning of rare words

Named after Mnemosyne, the Greek goddess of memory and mother of the muses, mnemonics have been used throughout history to assist in memorizing

How to Use this Book

everything from poetry and scientific terms to formulas and card games. Pythagoras used mnemonic hieroglyphic numerals to represent ideas. Mnemonic aids have also helped countless learners of both native and foreign languages. Many of us learned the rhyming i-before-e rule to assist with spelling, and some young children are taught to spell *together* and *attendance* by breaking them down into "to get her" and "at ten dance."

The mnemonic links contained in this book are meaning-mnemonics: each builds a bridge to the word's definition and provides a key to unlocking its meaning. Occasionally they assist in memorizing pronunciation as well, as in **ocean** for **otiant**. Even more rarely, they assist with spelling, the way the mnemonics for **peripeteia** and **peripatetic** draw attention to the difference in the two spellings. But more often, our mnemonics—like most puns and wordplays—take advantage of similarities with nonidentical words. Take care, then, that the mnemonics don't mislead as far as spelling and pronunciation. We recommend saying each word aloud before memorizing its mnemonic (see the key to our simple phonetic pronunciation system).

We hope these techniques help you remember rare words and relish using them.

Pronunciation Key and Abbreviations

Pronounced	As in
a	mat
$\bar{a}$ or ay	day
ah or o	hot
aw	law or more
b	boy
ch	chin
d	day
e or eh	pet
ee	feed
f	fill
g	go
h	hot
$\bar{i}$	hide
i or ih	kiss or agent
j	joy
k	kitten
l	lad
m	mad
n	not
ng	sing
$\bar{o}$	hope
o	hot
oi	boy
oo	boo
ou	out
p	pan
r	run
s or ss	yes
sh	shine
t	tin
th	thing
u or uh	run
ur	hurt
v	vote
y	young
z	zoo
zh	Asia

Pronunciation Key and Abbreviations

The pronunciation appears in parentheses following each word. Syllables are separated by hyphens. The accented syllable appears in large capital letters, the nonaccented syllables in lower case. In words with two accented syllables, the secondary accent appears in smaller caps (e.g., **animadversion**: AN-im-ad-VUR-zhun).

Guide to Abbreviations

adj.	adjective
adv.	adverb
e.g.	for example (Latin: *exempli gratia*)
esp.	especially
etc.	and so forth (Latin: *et cetera*)
i.e.	that is (Latin: *id est*)
n.	noun
n.pl.	noun plural
ult. [from]	ultimately [from]†
usu.	usually
v.i.	intransitive verb (no direct object—e.g., "I walked")
v.t.	transitive verb (takes a direct object—e.g., "I threw the ball")
v.i., v.t.	verb can be both intransitive and transitive (e.g., "I walked" or "I walked the dog")

† Indicates that one or more steps in a word's etymology have been skipped for brevity's sake. For example, **drupe**, an English word meaning fleshy pitted fruit, is from the Latin *drupa*, for overripe olive, which is from the Greek *druppa*, for olive. One can skip the Latin and say that drupe is ult. from the Greek *druppa*, for olive.

Alphabetical Listing of Words by Category

Numbers refer to page numbers.

Each word appears in its most appropriate category or categories. For example, **trophic** (pertaining to nutrition) appears in both *Food and Drink* and *Body and Medicine*.

Words with two or more meanings appear in each applicable category. For example, **turbinate** appears in both *Shape and Color* (as in spiraled or cone-shaped) and *Movement and Time* (as in to spin; whirl).

There are two general categories: *Action and Rest* and *Quality and Kind*, for words that do not fit into more specific categories.

Categories

Action and Rest

Architecture and Artifacts

Body and Medicine

Books and Publishing

Crime and Punishment

Death and Beyond

Existence and Essence

Food and Drink

Imagination and Emotions

Language and Speech

Learning and Knowledge

Logic and Argument

Manners and Dress

Military and Sports

Movement and Time

Music and the Arts

Nature and Matter

Order and Disorder

Place and Relation

Plants and Animals

Politics and Finance

Quality and Kind

Quantity and Measure

Romance and Sexuality

Shape and Color

Sight and Light

Social Groups and Relationships

Spirituality and Beliefs

Touch and Smell

Traits and Tendencies, Negative

Traits and Tendencies, Positive and Neutral

Words by Category

Action and Rest

bewray	78
cunctation	38
derogate	73
endue	28
fodient	73
furbish	74
fustigate	31
imbue	29
impetrate	36
obsecrate	36
otiant	18
poiesis	31
pretermit	34
proreption	66
revehent	22
sedulous	69

Architecture and Artifacts

bilbo	26
clinquant	39
empennage	69
fosse	45
glyph	51
haha	39
koftgari	23
ormolu	23
orrery	71
Palladian	67
parure	62
virtu	81

Body and Medicine

amygdala	25
apical	83
assuetude	41
blepharal	38
caducity	43
catabasis	27
claudicant	84
costive	56
crepitate	67
deric	62
diaphoresis	80
ectopia	80
embouchure	65
emesis	72
emetic	72
endogenous	35
etiology	33
exogenous	35
exuviate	63
fauces	45
fistulous	53
hebetic	55
homunculus	42
jugal	65
luxate	59
meatus	38
metopic	57
micturition	80
mithridatism	49
monoecious	43
nictitate	38
ochlesis	24
parietal	49
philtrum	57
recrement	80
rictus	77
risorial	46
roborant	60
secern	42
sinciput	57
spall	36
stenotic	62
sthenic	37
stocious	44
stomatic	77
strabismic	40

Words by Category

Words by Category

Words by Category

hamartiology 81
Hegelian 30
hermeneutic 55
heuristic 24
lucubrate 42
maieutic 61
Manichean 50
nescient 40
noetic 32
ontological 53
palinoia 65
Palladian 67
parviscient 40
peripatetic 21
phrontistery 40
plutology 27
prescient 40
sciolism 24
solipsism 68
thaumatology 55

Logic and Argument

apodictic 26
aposterioristic 33
aprioristic 33
casuistry 35
doxastic 69
elench 82
eristic 78
gravamen 49
quiddity 29
quoddity 29

Manners and Dress

adonize 78
agrestic 59
asteism 78
bilbo 26
caparison 30
charientism 78
consuetude 41

fustian 31
mansuetude 42
ormolu 23
parure 62
periapt 60
postiche 22
rabato 81
rebozo 81
selvage 25
soigné 55
solecism 69
sprezzatura 48
tiffany 74
webster 33

Military and Sports

aleatory 53
anabasis 27
catabasis 27
dimication 27
Fabian 45
kemp 29
pendragon 29
proreption 66
venery 60

Movement and Time

claudent 84
cursorial 20
eloign 43
enate 24
gressorial 20
hegira 37
jounce 74
novercal 84
olamic 63
orchesis 24
ortive 34
peripatetic 21
pridian 48

Words by Category

Words by Category

concinnity 20
desinence 84
distal 26
enchorial 60
endogenous 35
exogenous 35
fixity 82
Hesperian 34
incommensurable 74
lacuna 54
luxate 59
ortive 34
parallax 68
pensile 74
predial 62
procerity 42
purlieu 71
remanent 27
secant 47
secern 42
syndetic 21
ubiety 62

Plants and Animals

acaroid 30
anadromous 23
anlage 28
apatetic 72
atavism 28
axenic 18
catadromous 23
cervine 56
colubrine 81
columbine 81
commensal 74
conger 78
cursorial 20
drupe 19
dulosis 63
endogenous 35

exogenous 35
exuviate 63
fabaceous 30
fagaceous 30
fustic 37
gressorial 20
inquiline 74
lupine 46
nematode 57
nematoid 57
ovine 46
patulous 82
pensile 74
pileated 70
rasorial 46
roborean 60
roric 72
saurian 77
scopulate 52
sere 51
sericeous 51
solanaceous 19
telarian 32
urticate 64
venery 60
vulpine 46
zoetic 26

Politics and Finance

autarchy 73
claque 77
demit 65
dotation 31
dulocracy 63
dulosis 63
emption 49
endue 28
Fabian 45
kakistocracy 38
kleptocracy 38

11

Words by Category

muniments	66
obolary	27
pendragon	29
pignorate	38
plutology	27
predial	62
quietus	50
satrap	73
satyagraha	43

Quality and Kind

allicient	45
alterity	30
amyctic	30
amyous	81
antaean	41
apposite	43
assuasive	42
axenic	18
bootless	67
caducity	43
colletic	17
condign	68
congener	26
costive	56
divers	71
execrable	49
exigent	66
fatiferous	79
fuliginous	61
fusty	31
henotic	22
hylic	84
inanition	23
ineluctable	65
infandous	68
limbate	25
meable	38
muricate	64
nugatory	67

paludal	40
petrous	45
piceous	42
pistic	37
privative	59
roborean	60
sui generis	25
supererogatory	68
Tempean	65
venial	57

Quantity and Measure

aliquot	25
derogate	73
entropy	39
exiguous	66
incommensurable	74
nimiety	43
procerity	42
suppletion	62
ullage	23

Romance and Sexuality

allicient	45
anacreontic	71
apomixis	37
basial	17
Dionysian	39
frottage	82
gamic	37
ganosis	17
hebetic	55
monoecious	43
perfervid	66
prurient	32
rabelaisian	60
saturnalia	76
scopophilia	35

Words by Category

Words by Category

chiromancy 67
doxastic 69
empyrean 31
eschatology 18
Gnostic 51
hamartiology 81
hegira 37
Manichean 50
numinous 34
olamic 63
orphic 55
periapt 60
pistic 37
prelapsarian 52
protean 59
satori 72
satyagraha 43
tantric 22
thaumatology 55
thaumaturgic 55
theodicy 24
theophany 75

Touch and Smell

effluvium 71
haptic 30
mephitic 47
muricate 64
pruritic 32
urticate 64

Traits and Tendencies, Negative

acedia 50
apistia 82
Bacchant 44
captious 44
cyprian 77
epigone 43

eristic 78
esurient 29
execrable 49
fastuous 45
fatuous 45
frotteur 82
fulsome 61
fustian 31
fusty 31
grobian 76
gulosity 29
hamartia 81
hebetude 55
impudicity 34
inficete 54
invidious 63
Laodicean 54
lenocinant 17
louche 40
lumpen 58
maenad 52
manqué 62
minatory 18
misoneism 42
morigerous 54
mulierose 76
mumpsimus 38
Myrmidon 48
obscurant 83
orgulous 65
postiche 22
procacity 47
Procrustean 84
prurient 32
recreant 71
revanchist 81
stocious 44
strabismic 40
sumpsimus 38
tetricity 44

Words by Category

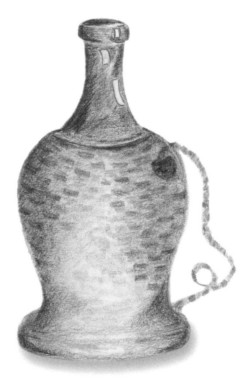

"I had the **chia**nti; then the chianti had me."

(See **chiasmus,** page 34)

Rare WORDS

1. **incunabula** (in-kuh-NAB-yuh-luh)

   n.pl. 1. primary stages of anything; beginnings; cradle period; infancy; origin. 2. books printed before A.D. 1500.

   ✧ **Incan**s existed before A.D. 1500, and so did incunabula.

2. **eidetic** (ī-DET-ik)

   adj. involving vivid recall of visual images.

   ✧ The **eye** recalls an eidetic image.

3. **ganosis** (guh-NŌ-siss)

   n. reducing sheen on marble, esp. on nude parts of statues (practiced in classical antiquity—an early form of censorship).

4. **colletic** (kuh-LET-ik)

   adj. adhesive. *n.* an adhesive substance, like glue.

   ✧ A colletic **collec**ts whatever it comes in contact with.

5. **neanic** (nee-AN-ik)

   adj. young; childlike.

   ✧ "I was just a child on my father's **knee**."

6. **lenocinant** (len-AH-sih-nunt)

   adj. lewd; lascivious.

   ✧ **Len**ny Bruce's m**o**nologues were often lenocinant.

7. **basial** (BAY-zee-uhl)

   adj. pertaining to kissing.

   ✧ ***Besa****me mucho* means kiss me a lot.

8. **paronym** (PAR-uh-nim)

   n. a word with the same root or derivation as that

of another word, either in the same or a different language (e.g., basial is a paronym of *besame*, and vice versa).

✧ A **pair of nam**es could be paronyms.

paronomasia (PAR-uh-nuh-MAY-zhyuh)

n. punning; a play on words.

✧ "This pun is so bad, it'll **amaze ya**."

9. **minatory** (MIN-uh-tawr-ee)

adj. menacing or mean.

✧ **Mean**-atory.

10. **eschatology** (ess-kuh-TOL-uh-jee)

n. the study of final things, including death, the afterlife and the end of the world (in Hebrew, *eeska* is the Hebrew prayer for the dead, although there is no known etymological relation).

11. **axenic** (ā-ZEN-ik)

adj. uncontaminated; germ-free.

✧ Axenic can be hygi**enic**.

12. **otiant** (ŌSH-yunt)

adj. idle; resting; unemployed.

✧ "With no wind, the sailboat lay otiant in the **ocean**."

13. **sennet** (SEN-it)

n. a set of notes played on the trumpet to mark the exit or entrance of actors.

14. **coruscate** (KAWR-us-kāt)

v.i. to glitter or gleam in flashes.

✧ "**Chorus skate**s brilliantly!"—a possible review of the Ice Capades.

nitid (NIT-id)

adj. shining; lustrous (ult. from the Latin *nitere*, to shine; shares a root with neat, which is a variant of the Anglo-Norman *neit*, meaning clear or pure).

✧ "She **knitted** a nitid sweater with metallic yarn."

15. **solanaceous** (sō-lun-AY-shuss)

adj. pertaining to peppers, tomatoes, eggplants or other plants of the nightshade family.

drupe (DROOP)

n. a fleshy fruit, such as the peach, plum or cherry, usu. with a single hard pit (ult. from the Greek *druppa*, for olive).

✧ Often, drupes **droop** on the tree because the pits are so heavy.

16. **proem** (PRŌ-em)

n. a preface.

exordium (eks-AWR-dee-um)

n. the opening portion of a speech or other writing.

17. **Delphic** (DEL-fik)

adj. vague; ambiguous (after the ancient oracle at Delphi, noted for giving ambiguous answers to questions).

18. **avatar** (AV-uh-tar)

n. the manifestation of a god on earth; an embodiment or concrete manifestation of an abstract concept (in Hindu mythology, the descent of a deity to earth in human or some other form).

✧ **Avia**tors descend to earth so frequently, they could be considered avatars!

19. **concinnity** (kon-SIN-it-ee)

n. 1. a skillful, harmonious arrangement of parts. 2. elegance of literary style.

eutaxy (YOO-tuk-see)

n. a harmonious arrangement.

20. **panegyric** (pan-uh-JEER-ik)

n. a speech of high praise; eulogy.

21. **gressorial** (grih-SAWR-ee-ul)

adj. adapted for walking (from the Latin past participle of *gradior, gradi,* to walk; the same root as congress, literally, "have come together").

cursorial (cur-SAWR-ee-ul)

adj. adapted for running.

✧ "That **cursor real**ly runs across my computer screen!"

22. **detritus** (dih-TRĪ-tus)

n. rubble; debris.

detrition (dih-TRISH-un)

n. erosion by friction.

23. **peripatetic** (pehr-ih-puh-TET-ik)

    adj. 1. walking or wandering around; traveling; itinerant. 2. pertaining or subscribing to the teachings of Aristotle. *n.* 1. a walking person; an itinerant. 2. a follower of Aristotle (from the Greek, literally, "walking around": Aristotle would walk around while lecturing to his students).

    ✧ **Perry**'s **pat**ter of wandering feet.

    peripeteia (pehr-ih-pih-TAY-uh)

    n. a sudden change in events, esp. in a dramatic work. (In O. Henry's "Gift of the Magi," the husband secretly pawns his watch and the wife cuts off and sells her hair so that each can buy the other a Christmas gift. Their gifts of a watch chain and a silver comb signal a peripeteia.)

    ✧ In **peri**l, **Pet**er Pan grows up—a dramatic turnaround.

24. **allantoid** (uh-LAN-toid)

    adj. sausage-shaped.

    lenticular (len-TIK-yuh-lur)

    adj. lentil-shaped.

25. **prosody** (PRAH-suh-dee)

    n. 1. the study of the metrical structure of verse. 2. a particular system of versification (as in: my love/is like/a red/red rose).

26. **syndetic** (sin-DET-ik)

    adj. 1. serving to connect or unite; copulative; conjunctive. 2. connected by a conjunction.

    ✧ Some **sin**s are syndetic in nature.

27. postiche (pō-STEESH)

n. 1. something fake. 2. a small hairpiece, toupée (from the Italian *posticcio*, for counterfeit).

✧ A **pos**eur is a postiche.

28. ligulate (LIG-yoo-lāt)

adj. lobe- or tongue-shaped (from the Latin *ligula*, for little tongue).

29. irenic (ī-REN-ik)

adj. promoting peace; conciliatory.

✧ "**Iren**e exhibits no ire."

henotic (heh-NOT-ik)

adj. promoting harmony or peace.

✧ If you think chickens are henotic, then you should start a **hen**harmo**nic**!

30. xeric (ZEHR-ik)

adj. of or adapted to dry environments.

✧ **Zero** precipitation.

31. tantric (TAHN-trik)

adj. pertaining to sacred sex (or other) practices grounded in the Tantra, a class of mystical Sanskrit texts.

32. revenant (REV-ih-nunt)

n. a person returning after death or a long absence; a ghost. *adj.* 1. ghostly; returning. 2. remembering something long forgotten.

revehent (REV-ih-hunt)

adj. carrying back (e.g., veins are revehent because they carry blood back to the heart).

✧ "We're revehent; we're carrying **Rover** back from the **hunt**."

33. **anadromous** (uh-NAD-ruh-muss)

    adj. going up-river from the sea to spawn (the Greek prefix *ana* means up; *dromos* means running).

    catadromous (kuh-TAD-ruh-muss)

    adj. going down-river to spawn in the sea (the Greek prefix *kata* means down).

34. **macarism** (MAK-uh-riz-um)

    n. pleasure in another's happiness (an antonym for schadenfreude, pleasure in another's misfortune).

35. **ormolu** (AWR-muh-loo)

    n. brass that resembles gold in furniture, architecture and jewelry.

    ✧ Ormolu is m**ore** like ore.

    koftgari (koft-gah-REE)

    n. the inlaying of steel with gold or silver (ult. from the Farsi, literally, "[gold]beating-craft").

36. **ullage** (UL-ij)

    n. the amount by which a container is less than full (due to leakage, evaporation or use).

    ✧ If there is ullage, it's less than f**ull**.

    inanition
    (in-un-ISH-un)

    n. 1. emptiness; the state or quality of being empty. 2. lack of physical or mental vitality (ult. from the Latin *inanis*, empty, and the same root as inane).

37. **theodicy** (thee-OD-ih-see)

n. a vindication of divine justice in the face of evil; an argument that God is good even though bad things happen (the word first appeared as the title of a work by the eighteenth-century German philosopher Gottfried Wilhelm Leibniz). Is **The Odyssey** theodicy? Possibly. In Homer's epic poem, Penelope's evil suitors have the run of Odysseus's home while he is adrift at sea, but the goddess Athena ensures that he eventually returns and sends his unwelcome houseguests to the underworld.

38. **ochlesis** (ō-KLEE-siss)

n. an unhealthy condition due to overcrowding.

orchesis (awr-KEE-siss)

n. the act of dancing; a rhythmical moving of the body.

✧ Orchesis is often **orch**estrated by a choreographer.

39. **sciolism** (SĪ-uh-LIZ-um)

n. pretense to wisdom or conceit due to wisdom.

40. **enate** (EE-nāt; ih-NĀT)

adj. growing outward.

enatic (ih-NAT-ik)

adj. related on the mother's side; having the same mother. n. a relative on the mother's side.

41. **heuristic** (hyoor-ISS-tik)

adj. leading to discovery, esp. through trial and error (the same root as "eureka," which means "I have discovered [it]" in Greek; often used to describe computer programs that learn from experience using trial and error rather than a rigid algorithmic approach).

✧ Dr. **Huer** was the brilliant discoverer in *Buck Rogers*.

42. **selvage** (SEL-vij)

n. the edge of woven fabric, finished to prevent unraveling.

✧ **Salv**age the **edge** and it will save the fabric.

limbate (LIM-bāt)

adj. having a border, esp. of a different color.

43. **sui generis** (SOO-ee JEN-ur-us)

adj. unique; in a class by itself (Latin for "of its own kind").

44. **amygdala** (uh-MIG-duh-luh) **amygdalae**

n., n.pl. 1. any almond-shaped bodily formation, such as the tonsils. 2. the almond-shaped mass of gray matter in the brain that regulates the body's fear response.

✧ **Amidala**, the queen played by Natalie Portman in the *Star Wars* series, often wears two amygdala-shaped ornaments on her ears. She was such a fearsome fighter, her fearful foes' amygdalae were often stimulated.

45. **rugate** (ROO-gāt)

adj. wrinkled.

✧ A **rug** is sometimes rugate.

46. **aliquot** (AL-ih-kwut)

n. an equal share; a number contained an exact number of times in another number (3 is an aliquot of 6). *v.t., v.i.* to divide into equal parts.

✧ **All equa**l parts of a number are its aliquots.

47. **zoetic** (zō-ET-ik)

adj. pertaining to life.

⟡ A **zo**o is zoetic—full of animal life.

48. **bilbo** (BIL-bō)

n. a sword (after the city of Bilbao in Spain, historically known for its well-tempered blades).

bilbo

n. an iron bar with foot shackles (origin unrelated; possibly from the Old French *boie*, for fetter).

49. **congener** (KON-jin-ur)

n. a thing or person of the same kind or class as another.

⟡ Congeners are **con**nected by **gen**us.

50. **zarf** (ZAHRF)

n. a cup-shaped device for holding hot coffee cups, usu. made of metal (from the Arabic *zarf*, for container).

51. **distal** (DISS-tul)

adj. away from the point of attachment or axis.

⟡ **Dista**nt from the axis.

52. **apodictic** (ap-uh-DIK-tik)

adj. undeniably or demonstrably true.

⟡ It is apodictic that **Dick** Nixon was **ap**t to lie about Watergate.

53. **oecist** (EE-sist)

n. a colonist.

⟡ Go **Eas**t, not **West**, young man, and colonize.

54. **docity** (DAH-sih-tee)

n. ability to learn quickly.

55. **plutology** (ploo-TOL-uh-jee)

n. the study of wealth.

obolary (AH-bō-lār-ee)

adj. extremely poor.

✧ A h**obo** is often obolary.

56. **remeant** (REE-mee-unt)

adj. returning.

✧ "I'm **re**turning to **me aunt**'s house."

remanent (REM-un-unt)

adj. remaining; residual.

✧ That which **rema**i**n**s is remanent.

remanet (REM-uh-nut)

n. postponement of a case (Latin for "it remains").

✧ "We'll **re**turn to this case in a **minut**e."

57. **dimication** (dim-ih-KAY-shun)

n. a fight or contest.

58. **anabasis** (uh-NAB-uh-siss)

n. a military expedition (the Greek warrior and writer Xenophon used this word, literally, "going up," to describe the Persian/Greek expedition across Asia Minor).

✧ **A** land **nab** is **a** ba**sis** for an anabasis.

catabasis (kuh-TAB-uh-siss)

n. 1. the retreat of an army (Xenophon recounted the Greek military retreat in his Anabasis). 2. a decline in the progress of a disease; remission.

✧ To **cut** out is **a basis** for catabasis.

59. **rubric** (ROO-brik)

n. 1. a title page, chapter heading or other part of a manuscript or page, often printed in red. 2. a class or category. *v.t.* to mark in red or arrange in a group.

✧ **Rub**y-**re**d type.

erubescent (er-oo-BESS-int)

adj. reddening.

rutilant (ROO-tul-unt)

adj. bright red.

60. **anlage** (on-LOG-uh)

n. inherited disposition to certain traits or a particular character development.

✧ Anlage is the **lugga**ge of inherited traits.

atavism (AT-uh-VIZ-um)

n. the reappearance of characteristics after skipping one or more generations; reversion to an earlier type ("like grandfather, like grandson").

61. **endue** (en-DOO; -DYOO)

v.t. to endow, as with honors or property; put on; invest, clothe; imbue.

imbue (im-BYOO)

v.t. to soak; dye; permeate.

62. **contronym** (KON-truh-nim)

n. a word with two or more contrary meanings, making it its own antonym (e.g., bolt means to flee but also means to secure).

✧ A contronym **contra**dicts itself.

63. **quiddity** (KWID-ih-tee)

n. 1. the essence of a thing. 2. a quibble; hairsplitting distinction (quiddity is a contronym).

quoddity (KWOD-ih-tee)

n. a quiddity (rare alternative; usu. used in conjunction with quiddity, as in "quiddities and quoddities").

64. **pendragon** (pen-DRAG-un)

n. a chief leader; head; dictator (originally, the title of a Celt war leader; King Arthur's father was named Uther Pendragon).

kemp (KEMP)

n. a champion warrior or athlete (originally, the winner of a harvesting contest in Scotland and Northern England).

65. **gulosity** (goo-LAH-sih-tee)

n. greediness; excessive appetite (from the Latin *gula*, for gluttony, one of the seven deadly sins).

✧ A gulosity for **goula**sh.

esurient (ih-SOOR-ee-int)

adj. voracious; greedy. *n.* such a person.

✧ **Esau** was so esurient, he sold his birthright to Jacob for a mess of pottage.

66. **Hegelian** (heh-GAY-lee-un)

adj. 1. pertaining to analysis using Hegel's dialectic of thesis, antithesis and synthesis. 2. pertaining to the philosophy of Hegel.

67. **alterity** (all-TEHR-ih-tee)

n. the state of being different.

✧ An **alter**ed state is different from the norm.

68. **caparison** (kuh-PAR-ih-sun)

n. a costume; ornamented clothes; trappings.
v.t. to place such coverings upon.

✧ A caparison can be a **cap**e for a horse or human.

69. **deliquesce** (del-ih-KWESS)

v.i. to melt away; dissolve by absorbing moisture in the air.

70. **haptic** (HAP-tik)

adj. pertaining to the sense of touch (haptics is a branch of psychology that studies sensations such as touch, temperature and pressure).

71. **fagaceous** (fuh-GAY-shuss)
adj. pertaining to the beech family of trees.

fabaceous (fuh-BAY-shuss)
adj. bean-like.

✧ **Fava** beans are fabaceous.

72. **amyctic** (uh-MIK-tik)
adj. irritating; itchy.

✧ **A mi**te or **tick** is amyctic.

acaroid (AK-uh-roid)
adj. mite- or tick-shaped.

73. dotation (dō-TAY-shun)

n. an endowment.

✧ England's Elizabeth I **dot**ed on Sir Walter Raleigh and his explor**ation**s, endowing him with money.

74. fustian (FUSS-tyun)

n. 1. pretentious or pompous language. 2. coarse cotton cloth. *adj.* 1. pompous. 2. good-for-nothing. 3. made of fustian.

✧ A fustian man holds his **fussed chin** high.

fustigate (FUSS-tih-gāt)

v.t. 1. to beat with a cudgel. 2. to criticize harshly (ult. from the Latin *fustis*, for cudgel or stick).

✧ "Anyone too **fast at** the **gate** will be fustigated."

fusty (FUSS-tee)

adj. 1. musty; moldy. 2. old-fogyish (from the Old French *fusté*, for tasting of the cask, ult. from the Latin *fustis*, for stick).

✧ A fuddy-duddy is **fusty**-musty.

75. poiesis (pō-EE-siss)

n. creative power; creation.

✧ Writing a **poe**m **is** an act of poiesis.

76. margaric (mar-GAR-ik)

adj. pearly. (The name Margaret means pearl.)

77. empyrean (em-PEER-ee-un)

n. the highest heaven. *adj.* pertaining to the highest heaven.

78. **agathism** (AG-uh-THIZ-um)

n. the belief that everything tends toward an ultimate good.

Panglossian (pan-GLOSS-ee-un)

adj. optimistic regardless of the circumstances (after Pangloss, the sunny tutor in Voltaire's *Candide*).

79. **oneiric** (o-NĪ-rik)

adj. pertaining to dreams.

80. **Daphnean** (DAF-nee-un)

adj. bashful. (Daphne was a Greek nymph who escaped Apollo by turning into a laurel tree.)

81. **insulse** (in-SULSS)

adj. tasteless; flat; insipid (from the Latin *insulsus,* literally, "unsalted").

82. **pruritic** (proo-RIT-ik)

adj. pertaining to itching, esp. without visible cause (from the Latin *prurire,* to itch, desire; the same root as prurient).

✧ Prur-**itch**-ic.

prurient (PROOR-ee-unt)

adj. fixated on sex; pertaining to or characterized by an obsessive interest in sex.

83. **noetic** (nō-ET-ik)

adj. given to purely intellectual or abstract reasoning; apprehended only by the intellect.

✧ If it's noetic, one can **know it** only
via intell**ect**.

84. **telarian** (tel-LĀR-ee-un)

adj. spinning a web. *n.* a webmaking spider. (*Tela* is Spanish for cloth or web.)

webster (WEB-stur)

n. a weaver.

✧ "Oh, what a tangled **web** we weave."

85. **catachresis** (kat-uh-KREE-siss)

n. 1. incorrect use of a word or phrase, esp. from an etymological misunderstanding. 2. strained use of a word or phrase, as for rhetorical effect. 3. a deliberately paradoxical figure of speech (ult. from the Greek *katakhresthai*, to misuse).

✧ To pronounce catachresis as "**cat**s **a**re **crease-sick**" is catachresis.

86. **aprioristic** (ā-prī-awr-ISS-tik)

adj. based on reasoning from principles rather than experience.

aposterioristic (ā-poss-TEE-ree-awr-ISS-tik)

adj. based on knowledge gained from experience; empirical.

87. **cantillate** (KAN-til-āt)

v.t., v.i. to chant or recite in a musical monotone, as in Hebraic or other rituals.

✧ "I **can** chant **till late**."

88. **etiology** (ee-tee-OL-uh-jee)

n. the study of causes, esp. of diseases.

✧ Etiology examines whether **eat**ing **all** fatty foods can cause heart disease.

89. **Hesperian** (heh-SPEHR-ee-un)

adj. western.

ortive (AWR-tiv)

adj. 1. eastern. 2. rising.

boreal (BAWR-ee-ul)

adj. northern (after Boreas, the Greek god of the north wind).

austral (AW-struhl)

adj. southern.

⟡ **Austral**ia is in the austral hemisphere.

90. **numinous** (NOO-min-us)

adj. awe-inspiring; incapable of being described or understood; mysterious (from the Latin *numen*, a divine force ascribed to an object or being).

91. **pretermit** (pree-tur-MIT)

v.t. to overlook; neglect; pass over.

92. **chiasmus** (kī-AZ-muss)

n. a rhetorical inversion of the second of two parallel structures (after the shape of the Greek letter Chi, an X shape).

⟡ "I had the **chia**nti; then the chianti had me" is a chiasmus.

93. **impudicity** (im-pyoo-DISS-ih-tee)

n. shamelessness.

⟡ "The **impud**ent child displayed his impudicity."

94. **palmary** (PAHL-muh-ree)

adj. prizeworthy; superior. (In ancient times, heroes were greeted with palms.)

95. **scopophilia** (skō-pō-FEEL-ee-uh)

    n. sexual stimulation derived from looking; voyeurism.

    ✧ The peeping Tom was caught **scop**ing **o**ut his neighbor.

96. **casuistry** (KAZH-oo-ist-ree)

    n. 1. the study of right and wrong; application of ethical rules to particular cases. 2. the false application of ethical principles; sophistry. (As with many terms pertaining to logic—e.g., quiddity and syllogistic—casuistry is a contronym [see 62].)

    ✧ The application of ethical rules to particular **cas**es is casuistry.

97. **syntomy** (SIN-tuh-mee)

    n. brevity; conciseness.

    ✧ "Syntomy in speech is no **sin to me**."

98. **endogenous** (en-DOJ-ih-nuss)

    adj. growing from within; originating within.

    ✧ Though Brooklyn lost its baseball team in 1953, many still claim the team as "**en-Dodger-nous**" to Brooklyn.

    exogenous (ek-SOJ-ih-nuss)

    adj. originating externally; due to external causes.

99. **thecate** (THEE-kāt)

    adj. sheathed; encapsuled.

100. *ben trovato* (ben-trō-VAH-tō)

    adj. appropriate even if untrue; well made up (often used as an exclamation to compliment a tall tale well told, from the Italian saying, *Se è non vero, è ben trovato*: "Even if it's not true, it is well made up").

101. impetrate (IM-pih-trāt)

> *v.t.* 1. to entreat; ask for. 2. to obtain by begging.

> ✧ It's a **pet trait** to impetrate treats.

obsecrate (OB-sih-krāt)

v.t. to implore; supplicate.

102. spall (SPAWL)

> *n.* a chip or fragment, esp. from a piece of stone or ore. *v.t.* to break up into small pieces. *v.i.* to chip or crumble (from *spalden*, the Middle English for "to split").

spall

> *n.* the shoulder (from the Latin *spatula*, meaning shoulder blade in Late Latin, flat piece of wood in Classical Latin; the same root as epaulette).

103. paralipsis (par-uh-LIP-siss)

> *n.* the emphasizing of something by affecting to pass it by without notice, usu. with such phrases as "not to mention" or "to say nothing of " (from the Greek *paraleipein*, to leave aside).

> ✧ "This **pair o' lips** won't utter a word about the secret rendezvous by **Sis**."

104. **onomastic** (ō-nō-MASS-tik)

    adj. pertaining to proper names or terms used in specialized fields; pertaining to the study of names.

    ✧ A book **on nam**es is onomastic.

105. **luteous** (LOO-tee-us)

    adj. mud- or clay-like; light or moderate greenish yellow.

    fustic (FUSS-tik)

    n. a tropical tree yielding yellow dye.

106. **hegira** (heh-JĪ-ruh), **hejira** (HEH-jih-ruh)

    n. flight; exodus (originally, the flight of Mohammed from Mecca in A.D. 622).

107. **sthenic** (STHEE-nik)

    adj. strong; robust; active; characterized by strength and activity of the muscular and nervous systems, esp. during illness (e.g., a sthenic fever).

    ✧ Sthenic suggests **streng**th.

108. **cozen** (KUZ-in)

    v.t. to deceive by fraud.

109. **pistic** (PISS-tik)

    adj. pure or pertaining to faith (from the Greek *pistikos*, for genuine, pure or faithful; from *pistis*, meaning faith or trust).

    ✧ The Ap**ost**les were pistic.

110. **gamic** (GAM-ik)

    adj. requiring mating or resulting from such.

    apomixis (ap-uh-MIK-siss)

    n. nonsexual reproduction.

111. **cunctation** (kunk-TAY-shun)

n. delay; procrastination.

112. **meatus** (mee-AY-tuss)

n. any body passage or opening of such a passage (as the ear canal).

meable (MEE-uh-bull)

adj. easily penetrable.

113. **whilom** (HWĪ-lum)

adv. formerly. *adj.* former.

✧ A**whil**e ago.

114. **kakistocracy** (KAK-iss-TOK-ruh-see)

n. government by the worst citizens (*kakistos* is Greek for worst).

kleptocracy (klep-TOK-ruh-see)

n. government by thieves.

115. **blepharal** (BLEF-ur-ul)

adj. pertaining to the eyelids.

✧ **Bl**inking is blepharal.

nictitate (NIK-tih-tāt)

v.i. to wink.

116. **pignorate, impignorate, opignorate** (PIG-nur-āt)

v.t. to pawn.

117. **sumpsimus** (SUMP-sih-muss)

adj. correct to a fault (e.g., "It Isn't Necessarily So" is a sumpsimus version of Gershwin's famous song, "It Ain't Necessarily So").

mumpsimus (MUMP-sih-muss)

n. 1. a bigot; one who adheres to a tenet or

custom regardless of evidence to the contrary.
2. a notion adhered to even though shown to
be unreasonable. (The word originated from
a priest of legend who incorrectly pronounced
sumpsimus as mumpsimus for thirty years.
When corrected, he said, "I'm not going
to change my mumpsimus for your new
sumpsimus!" His mumpsimus made him the
first mumpsimus.)

118. **entropy** (EN-truh-pee)

n. 1. measure of randomness; degree of disorder.
2. the steady, inevitable advance of a system or
society toward chaos. 3. the ultimate degradation
of the matter in the universe to a state of inertness.

119. **clinquant** (KLING-kunt; klang-KAHN)

adj. tinselled; glittering with tinsel or gold.
n. tinsel; imitation gold leaf.

✧ All that's clinquant isn't gold.

120. **haha** (HAH-hah)

n. a ditch with a wall inside that forms a
boundary without obstructing the view—so that
you see the ditch only when you've almost fallen
into it (formed by doubling *ha!*, the French
exclamation of surprise).

✧ "A**ha**! A haha!"

121. **Apollonian** (ap-ul-Ō-nee-un)

adj. 1. serene; rational; self-disciplined, like the
Greek god Apollo. 2. pertaining to the
mathematical works of Apollonius of Perga, esp.
his work on conic sections.

Dionysian (dī-uh-NISS-ee-un)

adj. orgiastic; sensual; inspired by instinct and
emotion, like Dionysius, the Greek god of wine
and fertility.

122. **paludal** (puh-LOO-dul)

adj. swampy.

✦ Paludal resembles **puddle**.

123. **enclitic** (en-KLIT-ik)

adj. leaning or dependent on a previous word with reference to accent or stress. *n.* a word or particle with no independent accent that attaches itself to the preceding word (e.g., the 'em in "go get 'em").

124. **undulant** (UN-jyuh-lunt)

adj. resembling waves; undulating.

125. **prescient** (PRESH-yint)

adj. having foreknowledge.

nescient (NESH-yint)

adj. lacking or disclaiming knowledge; agnostic.

✦ Nescience is **know**ledge **shunt**ed.

parviscient (par-VISH-ee-int)

adj. uninformed; having little knowledge.

126. **strabismic** (struh-BIZ-mik)

adj. 1. squinting or cross-eyed. 2. intellectually perverse (ult. from the Greek *strabismos*, a condition of squinting).

louche (LOOSH)

adj. dubious; suspicious; shady; disreputable (French for squinty-eyed or cross-eyed).

✦ **Louche**-y goosey.

127. **phrontistery** (fron-TISS-tur-ee)

n. a thinking-place; a place for meditation or study; a think tank (possibly coined by Aristophanes; in his play *The Clouds*, the lofty

Socrates lectures from a basket suspended from the ceiling with ropes and pulleys).

128. **antaean** (AN-tee-un)

adj. extremely powerful. (Antaeus was a wrestler who was invincible as long as he was touching the ground. Hercules lifted him and throttled him.)

✧ **Ant**s are antaean: they can carry many times their weight—as long as they're touching the ground.

129. **monition** (mō-NISH-un)

n. a caution; warning.

✧ **Monit**ors often issue monitions.

130. **consuetude** (KON-swih-tood)

n. 1. an established custom. 2. the book of customs and laws of an association.

assuetude (ASS-wih-tood)

n. the state of being accustomed, esp. to harmful influences. (According to Francis Bacon, "Assuetude of things hurtful doth make them lose their force to hurt.")

mansuetude (MAN-swih-tood)

n. gentleness of manner; mildness.

✧ A man with mansuetude has **man**ners and a **sweet** atti**tude**.

131. homunculus (hō-MUNG-kyoo-luss)

n. a little man or a human embryo. (Homunculus formerly referred to the miniature human that was believed to exist in the head of each sperm, according to the early biological theory of preformation.)

132. lucubrate (LOO-kyoo-brāt)

v.i. to study at night; "burn the midnight oil."

✧ A person who lucubrates **look**s at **b**ooks ve**ry** l**ate**.

133. piceous (PĪ-see-us; PIH-see-us)

adj. 1. pitch dark. 2. combustible, like pitch, which is a flammable, tar-like substance.

✧ "So **pit**eous you can't **see us** when it's piceous!"

134. secern (sih-SURN)

v.t. 1. to discriminate; separate. 2. to secrete.

✧ To secern is to di**scern**.

135. assuasive (uh-SWAY-siv)

adj. mitigating; tranquilizing; soothing.

✧ That which is assuasive **assua**ges.

136. procerity (prō-SER-ih-tee)

n. tallness; height.

137. misoneism (MISS-uh-NEE-iz-um)

n. hatred of change (literally, "hatred of new things").

✧ People afflicted with misoneism are happy to **miss a new -ism**.

138. **apposite** (AP-uh-zit)

adj. appropriate.

✧ Apposite means **apt**.

139. **nimiety** (nih-MĪ-ih-tee)

n. excess; redundancy.

140. **eudemonia** (yoo-dih-MŌ-nee-uh)

n. true happiness. (According to Aristotle's *Ethics*, eudemonia results from a life lived according to the dictates of reason.)

141. **monoecious** (muh-NEE-shuss)

adj. having both male and female organs; hermaphroditic.

✧ Monoecious means **man-is-she**.

142. **epigone** (EP-ih-gōn)

n. a second-rate imitator or follower, esp. of a philosopher or artist.

143. **satyagraha** (SUT-ya-GRUH-huh)

n. nonviolent noncooperation with evil; a policy of using nonviolent resistance to press for political reform, pioneered by Mahatma Gandhi and practiced by Martin Luther King Jr. and others (literally, "truth-firmness" in Sanskrit).

144. **caducity** (kuh-DOO-sih-tee)

n. 1. the frailty of old age. 2. impermanence.

145. **eloign** (ee-LOIN)

v.t. to remove; carry away to a distance; conceal.

✧ "Elaine was eloigned **a long** way."

146. **indite** (in-DĪT)

v.t. to write down; describe.

indict (in-DĪT)

v.t. to accuse of a crime or other offense.

147. **megrims** (MEE-grimz)

n.pl. state of nervous depression; "the dumps" (from the Middle English *megrim*, a variant of migraine).

✧ "**Me grim**. Me depressed."

148. **tmesis** (tuh-MEE-siss)

n. the insertion of one or more words into the middle of a compound word (e.g., "never ever more" instead of "nevermore").

149. **Bacchant** (BAK-unt)

n. a drunken reveler (originally, a priest, priestess or devotee of Bacchus, the Greek and Roman god of wine who was associated with Dionysius).

stocious (STŌ-shuss)

adj. drunk (Irish slang).

150. **captation** (kap-TAY-shun)

n. 1. an attempt to obtain applause, acceptance or recognition. 2. an attempt to control another's mind; hypnosis.

✧ A captation is an attempt to **capt**ure minds.

captious (KAP-shuss)

adj. 1. fault-finding. 2. calculated to entrap through subtlety.

✧ "The captious man tried to **capt**ure **us** in a lie."

151. **tetricity** (teh-TRISS-ih-tee)

n. austerity; harshness.

152. **Fabian** (FAY-bee-un)

adj. strategically cautious; seeking victory by delay rather than battle (after Q. Fabius Maximus, a Roman general who employed this strategy. The Fabian Society, founded in 1844, advocates gradual political change. George Bernard Shaw was a member).

153. **suberous** (SOO-bur-us), **suberose** (SOO-bur-ōss)

adj. corky; resembling cork.

petrous (PET-russ)

adj. stony.

154. **edacious** (ee-DAY-shuss)

adj. eating a lot; voracious.

✧ "The edacious teenagers **ea**t all **day**."

155. **fastuous** (FASS-choo-us)

adj. arrogant; showy.

fatuous (FATCH-oo-us)

adj. smugly foolish.

156. **riposte** (rih-PŌST)

n. a sudden and quick reply. *v.i.* to answer quickly.

157. **allicient** (uh-LISH-int)

adj. attracting. *n.* something that attracts.

✧ **Alice** Liddell was allicient to Lewis Carroll.

158. **fauces** (FAW-seez)

n. the passage from mouth to pharynx.

✧ The fauces is the **fauce**t of the body.

fosse (FAH-see)

n. a canal; ditch; trench.

159. **lupine** (LOO-pīn)

adj. wolf-like.

vulpine (VULL-pīn)

adj. fox-like.

ovine (Ō-vīn)

adj. sheep- or egg-like.

160. **demotic** (deh-MOT-ik)

adj. popular; pertaining to the common people.

✧ **Demo**cracy is demotic rule.

161. **appetence** (AP-ih-tinss)

n. strong desire or instinct; craving.

✧ One who possesses appetence has an **appe**tite for something.

162. **rasorial** (ruh-ZAWR-ee-uhl)

adj. given to scratching the ground for food, as chickens and similar birds do.

✧ A **razor** scratches, as do rasorial birds.

risorial (rih-ZAWR-ee-ul)

adj. producing laughter (e.g., the risorial muscles; *risa* means laughter in Spanish).

163. **procellous** (prō-SELL-us)

adj. stormy.

✧ Go to the **cell**ar when it's procellous.

164. **macaronic** (mak-uh-RON-ik)

adj. involving a mixture of two languages; jumbled (ult. from the dialectical Italian *maccaroni*, a dish of mixed food. An Italian Renaissance poet named Merlinus Cocceius coined the term to describe his verse, a jumble of Latin words and vernacular words with Latinate endings). *n.* a jumble; a verse or other composition using two or more languages.

165. **procacity** (prō-KASS-ih-tee)

n. insolence; pertness.

166. **mephitic** (meh-FIT-ik)

adj. terribly stinky.

✧ "Wherever **Mephis**to waltzes, it smells like hell."

167. **secant** (SEEK-unt; SEK-unt)

adj. cutting; dividing into two sections. *n.* a line that cuts another.

✧ The secant line, you **see, can** cut the circle in two, while the tangent line can only touch it.

168. **previse** (prih-VĪZ)

v.t. to foresee; notify in advance (literally, "see before").

cecity (SEE-sih-tee)

n. blindness (chiefly figurative; Oedipus was afflicted with cecity even before his eyes were gouged, since he was not aware that his wife was his mother).

✧ Those with cecity **cease to see**.

169. **scoptic** (SKOP-tik)

adj. mocking or satirical. *n.* such writing.

✧ Scoptic writing **scoff**s at things.

170. **potamic** (pō-TAM-ik)

adj. pertaining to rivers or river navigation.

✧ The **Potomac** is Washington's
potamic attraction.

fluminous (FLOO-min-uss)

adj. pertaining to rivers; having many rivers
or streams.

✧ A region where **fl**owing rivers are n**um**er**ous**
is fluminous.

171. **tessitura** (tess-ee-TOO-rah)

n. the general range of a melody or voice part in
a singing ensemble. The "Star-Spangled Banner"
has a broad tessitura.

sprezzatura (spret-sa-TOO-rah)

n. the art of doing a difficult thing so gracefully
that it looks easy; an appearance of ease and
nonchalance, even disdain. (In his sixteenth-
century *Book of the Courtier*, the Renaissance
manners maven Castiglione said that a gentleman
should have *sprezzatura*, an appearance of
aloofness and disdain.)

172. **pridian** (PRIH-dee-un)

adj. pertaining to yesterday or a previous day
(from the Latin *pridianus*, literally, "of the
day before").

✧ "**Pretty Ann**'s pridian tryst occupied
her thoughts."

173. **Myrmidon** (MUR-mih-duhn; MUR-mih-DON)

n. a faithful follower who carries out orders
without question; a minion. (The Myrmidons
were legendary Greek warriors who followed
their king Achilles in fighting against Troy.)

174. **gravamen** (gruh-VAY-men; gruh-VAH-men)

n. the gist of a grievance or charge; the most substantial part of an accusation.

✧ "For those grave men who ask what women's main **griev**ance is: it's equality. **Amen**!"

175. **emption** (EMP-shun)

n. the act of buying.

✧ *Caveat* **empt**or means buyer beware.

176. **mithridatism** (MITH-rih-DAY-tiz-um)

n. immunity from poison by taking a series of gradually increasing doses (after Mithridates VI, an ancient king who was reported to have acquired a tolerance to poison by doing so).

177. **pother** (PAH-thur)

n. disturbance; fuss.   *v.t.* to harass; trouble. *v.i.* to fuss (originally: a choking cloud of dust, smoke or steam).

✧ A pother is a b**other**.

178. **lowery** (LOU-ur-ee)

adj. cloudy; gloomy (as in a lowery sky).

179. **animadversion** (AN-im-ad-VUR-zhun)

n. a negative comment; criticism (literally, "pointing out with animus").

180. **parietal** (puh-RĪ-ih-tul)

adj. 1. forming the wall of a cavity. 2. pertaining to the bones that form the sides and top of the skull (*pared* means wall in Spanish).

181. **execrable** (EKS-ih-kruh-bull)

adj. loathsome.

✧ Ex-**ick**-rable.

182. **anomie, anomy** (AN-uh-mee)

n. 1. lawlessness or lack of social standards in a society or person. 2. a feeling of alienation or purposelessness in a person resulting from a lack of moral or social standards in society.

acedia (uh-SEE-dee-uh),
accidie (AK-ih-dee; AK-sih-dee)

n. a state of spiritual torpor; apathy; anomie (from the Latin *acedia*, one of the seven deadly sins, often translated as sloth; Chaucer referred to "the sin of accidie").

183. **preconize** (PREE-kun-īz)

v.t. to proclaim; publish.

184. **quietus** (kwī-EE-tus)

n. 1. death; release from life; something that serves to eliminate. 2. the settlement of an obligation or debt.

185. **mainour** (MAY-nur)

n. stolen goods found on a thief.

✧ "He was caught with the mainour, **main**ly **ore** from the manor."

pelf (PELF)

n. riches, esp. ill-gotten gains; booty.

✧ Pelf is usually **pilf**ered.

186. **Manichean** (man-ih-KEE-in)

adj. 1. pertaining to a dualistic, black-and-white worldview; pertaining to a belief in incessant warfare between good and evil. 2. renouncing things material and sensual as evil in origin and holding that wisdom is attained through asceticism. *n.* one who holds such beliefs; a dualist.

Gnostic (NAH-stik)

adj. pertaining to a belief in spiritual knowledge over faith; possessing intellectual or spiritual knowledge; cognitive. *n.* one who holds such beliefs. (Gnosticism was a philosophical and religious movement that valued inquiry into spiritual truth above faith.)

187. **sericeous** (sih-RISH-us)

adj. silky; covered with soft, silky hairs.

✧ **Si**lk, a **rich** fabric, is sericeous.

sere (SEER)

adj. withered; dry.

✧ In **sear**ing hot weather, plants become sere.

188. **glyph** (GLIF)

n. 1. a carved figure or any other symbol that imparts knowledge nonverbally, such as a school crossing sign. 2. a vertical groove, esp. in a Doric column or frieze (from the Greek *gluphein*, to carve).

ankh (AHNGK)

n. a T-shaped cross with a loop on top symbolizing both physical and eternal life (also known as an ansate—i.e., handle-possessing—cross; ankh is an ancient Egyptian symbol for the power to give and sustain life).

189. **prelapsarian** (pree-lap-SĀR-ee-un)

adj. pertaining to the period before Adam and Eve ate the apple and were banished from Eden.

✧ **Pre-lapse** with the apple, Adam and Eve had not a c**are**.

190. **clavate** (KLAY-vāt)

adj. club-shaped.

scopulate (SKOP-yuh-lāt)

adj. broom-shaped; brushlike.

bacillar (BASS-ih-lur),
bacillary (BASS-ih-LĀR-ee)

adj. rod-shaped.

✧ One can catch **bass** and other fish with bacillar gear.

191. **maenad** (MEE-nad)

n. a frenzied woman (also known as a Bacchante, a maenad was a female participant in orgiastic rites associated with the Greek god Bacchus; ult. from the Greek *mainesthai*, to rave, and the same root as mania).

192. **diapason** (dī-uh-PAY-sun; -zun)

n. 1. an outpouring of sound that is rich, deep and usu. harmonious; a loud burst of sound. 2. the entire range of something, esp. an instrument or voice. 3. the interval of an octave. 4. a main stop on a pipe organ that controls volume and extends through the complete range of the instrument. 5. a tuning fork (ult. from the Greek *diapason*, literally, "through all [the notes]").

⬦ One can pull out all the stops on a pipe organ, letting it all **play on**.

193. **aleatory** (ĀL-ee-uh-tawr-ee)

adj. pertaining to gambling; relying on chance.

194. **epistemic** (ep-ih-STEM-ik)

adj. relating to knowledge.

epistemological (eh-PIST-em-ul-OJ-ik-ul)

adj. pertaining to the study of knowledge.

ontological (ON-tuh-LOJ-ih-kul)

adj. pertaining to the study of being.

195. **adumbrate** (AD-um-brāt; uh-DUM-brāt)

v.t. 1. to make a silhouette; outline; sketch roughly. 2. to partially disclose. (ult. from the Latin *umbra*, a shade or shadow; TV news shows often adumbrate interview subjects who don't wish to be identified).

limn (LIM)

v.t. 1. to draw, paint or outline in sharp detail. 2. to describe; delineate; portray in words (ult. from the Latin *illuminare*, to illuminate).

196. **fistulous** (FISS-chuh-luss)

adj. 1. tubular and hollow. 2. resembling a fistula, an abnormal passage in the body caused by illness (from the Latin *fistula*, for pipe or flute).

⬦ A **fist** is fistulous; it creates a hollow.

197. **litotes** (LĪ-tuh-teez; lī-TŌ-teez)

n., n.pl. the use of understatement, esp. by negating a contrary statement (e.g., saying "not bad" to mean "good").

antiphrasis (an-TIH-fruh-siss)

n. a word used to mean its opposite (e.g., saying someone's "bad" to mean he or she is "good").

198. **morigerous** (mur-IJ-ur-us)

adj. obsequiously obedient.

✧ Someone morigerous is **more eager** to obey **us**.

199. **littoral** (LIT-ur-ul)

adj. pertaining to a seashore. *n.* a coastal region.

✧ "Don't **litter** the lovely littoral spot!"

200. **exequy** (EK-sih-kwee)
exequies

n., n.pl. a funeral ceremony.

✧ An exequy marks a person's **exi**t from this world.

201. **lacuna** (luh-KOO-nuh)
lacunae (luh-KOO-nī; -nay)

n., n.pl. 1. a gap; cavity; depression. 2. a gap in a text (*lacuna* is Latin for lagoon).

202. **Thalian** (thuh-LĪ-un)

adj. comic; pertaining to comedy.

✧ **The lion** in *The Wizard of Oz* is Thalian.

inficete (IN-fuh-seet)

adj. humorless; lacking in wit; unfunny.

✧ Inficete means **unfacet**ious.

203. **Laodicean** (lay-OD-ih-SEE-un)

adj. lukewarm or indifferent. (The early Christians of Laodicea, the ruins of which are in Turkey, were warned in the New Testament that they were indifferent to spiritual matters.)

204. hermeneutic (hur-mih-NOO-tik; -NYOO-tik), hermeneutical

adj. interpretive; explanatory. (Hermes was the envoy for the Greek gods.)

205. yclept (ee-KLEPT)

adj. named (e.g., the best-known bard is yclept William Shakespeare).

206. thaumatology (THAW-muh-TOL-uh-jee)

n. the study of miracles.

thaumaturgic (THAW-muh-TUR-jik)

adj. miraculous; magical; working miracles.

207. hirrient (HEER-ee-int)

adj. strongly trilled; rolled, as some forms of r.
n. a strongly or harshly trilled sound.

✧ One **hear**s a hirrient as "hirrrr-ient."

208. orphic (AWR-fik)

adj. mystical; magical; hypnotic; melodious. (The mythical Greek poet Orpheus cast spells with his singing, and the writings ascribed to him contained philosophical mysteries.)

209. soigné (swan-YAY)

adj. well-groomed; meticulously dressed; carefully prepared.

✧ Charles Swann in Proust's **Swann**'s **Way** was soigné.

210. hebetude (HEB-ih-tood)

n. dullness; lethargy (from the Latin *hebes*, dullness).

hebetic (heh-BET-ik)

adj. occurring at puberty (Hebe was a Greek goddess of youth and spring).

211. **costive** (KOSS-tiv)

adj. constipated or causing constipation; slow or reluctant in action.

212. **eremitic** (ehr-ih-MIT-ik), **eremitical**

adj. reclusive.

✧ A h**ermit** is eremitic.

farouche (fah-ROOSH)

adj. 1. wild; fierce. 2. shy; withdrawn; sullen (a contronym [see 62], farouche is ult. from the Late Latin *forasticus*, meaning belonging outdoors).

✧ When removed **far** from the wild, an un**ru**ly person can become **sh**y.

213. **cervine** (SUR-vīn)

adj. pertaining to deer.

✧ **Serve ven**ison.

cervisial (sur-VISS-ee-ul)

adj. pertaining to beer (from the Latin *cervisia*, meaning beer).

✧ "**Servis**h me a beer"—a request from one who's had one too many.

214. **venal** (VEE-null)

    adj. corruptible; mercenary; unscrupulous; open to bribery.

    venial (VEE-nee-ull)

    adj. forgivable; not criminal.

215. **scree** (SKREE)

    n. a steep slope with loose soil and stones.

    ✧ **Scre**am for help if you slip on a scree.

    screed (SKREED)

    n. a long harangue, either spoken or written.

    ✧ A screed is sometimes **scre**amed.

216. **nematoid** (NEM-uh-toid)

    adj. wormy; pertaining to the roundworm.

    nematode (NEM-uh-tōd)

    n. a kind of threadlike worm that is often parasitic.

217. **metopic** (mih-TOP-ik)

    adj. pertaining to the forehead.

    ✧ "**Me** forehead—the **top** of me face— is metopic."

    sinciput (SIN-sih-put)

    n. the frontal, upper part of the cranium, from the forehead reaching to the crown.

    ✧ "**Since I put** a cap on, you can't see my sinciput."

    philtrum (FIL-trum)

    n. the trough-like hollow in the middle of the upper lip, right beneath the nostrils.

    ✧ "If **Phil trim**s his moustache, his philtrum will be visible."

218. Barmecide (BAHR-mih-sīd)

n. a person who offers imaginary food or illusory benefits. *adj.* make-believe (as in Barmecide feast: Barmecide was a prince in *Arabian Nights* who served a beggar a feast of imaginary dishes and wine to test his humor; when the beggar played along, he was rewarded with a real feast).

✧ "A **bar**tender tried to serve **me** Barmecide drinks."

illude (ih-LOOD)

v.t. to deceive; play upon.

✧ To illude is to create an **illu**sion.

lusory (LOO-sur-ee)

adj. playful; used in play.

219. traduce (truh-DOOSS)

v.t. to slander; speak falsely or maliciously of.

220. lumpen (LUM-pin)

adj. 1. ignorantly contented. 2. boorish; stupid; raggedy. (*Lumpen* is German for rags. Karl Marx transformed the meaning of the word when he coined the term *lumpenproletariat* to refer to the poorest, least cohesive section of the working class.)

canaille (cun-Ī)

n. rabble; riffraff (a French word derived from the Italian *canaglia*, literally, "pack of dogs").

✧ *Cave canaille*: Beware the rabble.

221. talionic (tal-ee-ON-ik)

adj. retaliatory in exact measure—e.g., "an eye for an eye" (*lex talionis* was the Roman law of retaliation).

✧ Tit for **tal**ionic.

222. **orectic** (awr-EK-tik)

adj. pertaining to desires and their satisfaction (but the same root as anorexia, literally, "lack of appetite" in Greek).

anhedonia (an-hih-DŌN-ee-uh)

n. inability to enjoy things.

223. **privative** (PRIV-uh-tiv)

adj. 1. causing deprivation, lack or loss. 2. altering a word's meaning from positive to negative. *n.* 1. that which causes deprivation. 2. a prefix or suffix that changes a word's meaning from positive to negative—e.g., "non-" or "-less."

✧ The privative de**priv**es.

224. **anidian** (a-NIH-dee-un)

adj. shapeless; formless (ult. from the Greek *eidos*, for form, with the privative prefix "an-" added).

protean (PRŌ-tee-un)

adj. able to change shape or form (as did the Greek god Proteus).

225. **luxate** (LUK-sāt)

v.t. to throw out of joint; dislocate.

✧ To dis**locate** your shoulder is to luxate it.

226. **agrestic** (uh-GRESS-tik)

adj. 1. pertaining to fields; rural; rustic. 2. uncouth.

✧ **Agr**iculture is an agrestic art.

georgic (JAWR-jik)

adj. countrified; rural.

✧ **George** Washington was georgic: one of his greatest joys was farming.

227. **rabelaisian** (ra-buh-LAY-zee-un)

adj. coarse-humored; ribald (after François Rabelais, the sixteenth-century French author of *Gargantua and Pantagruel*, a raunchy romp).

✧ "The **rabble** was pleased with Rabelais' tales."

228. **venery** (VEN-ur-ee)

n. the act of hunting (ult. from the Latin *venari*, to hunt).

✧ Venery sometimes results in **veni**son.

venery

n. indulgence in sexual intercourse (ult. from the Latin *venus*, desire).

✧ Venery sometimes leads to **venere**al disease.

229. **roborant** (ROB-uh-runt)

adj. restorative. *n.* a healing tonic or drug.

roborean (ruh-BAWR-ee-un)

adj. 1. strong, like an oak. 2. made of oak.

✧ A **ro**borean ar**bor** is an orchard of oaks.

230. **periapt** (PEHR-ee-apt)

n. an amulet or charm worn as protection from disease or harm.

✧ Some say you're **apt** to be protected if you wear a periapt.

231. **jongleur** (zhon-GLOOR)

n. a storyteller; singer. (Jongleurs were Medieval French and English minstrels. Juggler shares the same Old French root as jongleur.)

232. **enchorial** (en-KAWR-ee-ul), **enchoric** (en-KAWR-ik)

adj. native to a particular country.

233. **fulgurate** (FUL-jur-āt)

v.t., v.i. to emit flashes. (*Fulgur* is Latin for lightning, believed to be caused by the Roman god Jupiter when he was angry.)

✧ When **Ju**piter is i**rate**, he fulgerates.

fuliginous (ful-IJ-ih-nuss)

adj. sooty (from the Latin *fuligo*, for soot).

✧ A **full ledge** of soot.

234. **maieutic** (may-OO-tik)

adj. pertaining to the Socratic method of coaxing a person's latent ideas to the forefront of his or her consciousness.

maieutics

n.pl. the Socratic method; mental midwifery (from the Greek *maieutikos*, "of midwifery").

235. **fulsome** (FUL-sum)

adj. loathsome; offensively flattering; cloying; insincere (literally, "excessively full").

✧ "He's **full** o' **some** baloney."

✧ **Foul**-some.

236. suppletion (suh-PLEE-shun)

n. the act of supplementing or supplying.

✧ The opposite of de**pletion** is suppletion.

237. parure (pah-ROOR)

n. a pair of gems.

✧ A **pair** of rhinestones **or** ruby earrings
is a parure.

238. stenotic (stih-NOT-ik)

adj. pertaining to the narrowing of a passage
or orifice.

✧ **Stan**ching is stenotic.

239. deric (DER-ik)

adj. pertaining to the skin.

✧ Deric ailments are treated by **der**matologists.

240. ubiety (yoo-BĪ-ih-tee)

n. location; position; state of being in a
certain place.

✧ "Wherever **you be**, there be **I**."

predial, praedial (PREE-dee-ul)

adj. pertaining to real estate; possessing or
involving landed property (ult. from the Latin
praedium, for landed property; in Europe's
Middle Ages, praedial serfs were considered part
of the land in real estate transactions).

✧ **Pre**-mortgage, one must make a predial **deal**.

241. manqué (mon-KAY)

adj. falling short of expectations; unrealized as
a goal; unfulfilled; frustrated (usu. placed after
the noun it modifies—e.g., artist manqué).

✧ **Monkey**s might be insulted to be called
humans manqué.

242. **antinomy** (an-TIN-ō-mee)

n. a paradox in which two contradictory principles are both correct.

antimony (an-TIH-muh-nee)

n. a brittle, silvery-white elemental metal used in batteries, fireproofing, paints and ceramics.

243. **olamic** (ō-LOM-ik)

adj. eternal; infinite (from the Hebrew *olam*, a vast period of time; an age in the universe).

244. **invidious** (in-VIH-dee-us)

adj. provoking envy or ill will.

◇ "Did his invidious preference for Sally invoke **envy** in **Dee**? **Yes**!"

245. **corrigendum** (kawr-ih-JEN-dum) **corrigenda**

n., n.pl. a printer's error to be corrected.

246. **exuviate** (ek-SOO-vee-āt)

v.t., v.i. to shed (skin); slough.

247. **threnody** (THREN-uh-dee)

n. a funeral song or poem; lamentation; dirge.

◇ A funeral **ode** is a threnody.

248. **dulosis** (doo-LŌ-siss)

n. enslavement, esp. of worker ants by ants of rival species.

dulocracy (doo-LOK-ruh-see)

n. government by slaves.

249. **causerie** (KŌ-zur-ee)

n. a piece of writing in a conversational tone.

◇ A causerie **cause**s cozy **rea**ding.

250. **aphesis** (AF-ih-siss)

n. loss of the unaccented vowel at the beginning of a word.

✧ To say '**phesis** for aphesis is aphesis.

apocope (uh-PAH-kuh-pee)

n. the cutting off of one or more letters or sounds at the end of a word.

✧ To say **apoc** for apocope is apocope.

251. **urticate** (UR-tih-kāt)

v.t. to sting, as with nettles (*urtica* is Latin for nettle).

✧ To urticate is to h**urt** by stinging.

muricate (MYUR-ih-kāt)

adj. prickly.

252. **villous** (VIL-us)

adj. shaggy-haired.

253. **antonomasia** (AN-tuh-nuh-MAY-zhuh)

n. 1. the use of a proper name as an epithet (e.g., referring to a handsome man as "a regular Antonio Banderas"). 2. the substitution of a title or epithet for a proper name (e.g., "Antonio is the Heartthrob of Hollywood").

254. **chrestomathy** (kress-TOM-uh-thee)

n. 1. a selection of literary passages or stories by an author. 2. an anthology used to help learn a language.

255. **trophic** (TRŌ-fik)

adj. pertaining to nutrition.

✧ A **trough** can contain trophic food.

256. **anaphora** (uh-NAF-ur-uh)

n. the deliberate repetition of a word in several successive clauses. (Presidents and preachers love anaphora: "We can not dedicate—we can not consecrate—we can not hallow this ground," wrote Abraham Lincoln in his Gettysburg Address.)

257. **embouchure** (OM-boo-SHOOR)

n. 1. the shape of the mouth when blowing on a musical instrument or the mouthpiece of a musical instrument. 2. the mouth of a river.

258. **Tempean** (tem-PEE-un; TEM-pee-un)

adj. beautiful and delightful (like the Tempe valley in Thessaly, Greece).

✧ "A **paean** to things Tempean."

259. **orgulous** (AWR-gyuh-luss)

adj. prideful; haughty.

260. **demit** (dih-MIT)

v.i., v.t. to relinquish an office or function.

✧ "Here's **de mitt**—I quit."

261. **palinoia** (pal-ih-NOI-uh)

n. compulsive repetition of an act until it is perfect; rote learning.

✧ "**Pa'll annoy ya** with rote. Pa'll annoy ya with rote. Pa'll annoy ya with rote."

262. **ineluctable** (in-ih-LUK-tuh-bul)

adj. unavoidable; inevitable.

263. **jugal** (JOO-gul)

adj. pertaining to the bony arch of the cheek (from the Latin *jugum*, yoke, and the same root as conjugal; literally, "of things yoked together").

264. perfervid (pur-FUR-vid)

adj. zealous; extremely fervid; burning with passion.

265. crepuscular (krih-PUSK-yuh-lur)

adj. dusk-like; dim.

✧ Crepuscular is d**usk**-ular.

266. seriatim (seer-ee-AY-tim)

adv. in a series; in regular order; one after another.

267. proreption (prō-REP-shun)

n. a sneak attack; secretive advance.

✧ The reptile c**rept** closer in a proreption.

268. muniments (MYOO-nih-mints)

n.pl. ownership papers; proof of ownership.

✧ The **muni**cipal building is the place to obtain muniments.

269. exiguous (ek-SIG-yoo-us)

adj. scanty; sparse; meager.

exigent (EK-sih-jint)

adj. requiring immediate attention; demanding; exacting.

✧ If it's exigent, it's ur**gent**.

270. crepitate (KREP-ih-tāt)

v.i. to crackle; burp; audibly emit gas.

271. apostrophize (uh-POSS-truh-FĪZ)

v.i. to digress; turn away from an audience; speak to an absent or imaginary person (ult. from the Greek *apostrophein*, literally, "to turn away").

272. chiromancy (KĪ-rō-man-see)

n. the art of palm-reading.

Chaldean (KAL-dee-un)

adj. referring to astrology or mysticism. (The Chaldeans were members of an ancient Semitic people who ruled in Babylonia, the ruins of which are in Iraq.)

273. nugatory (NOO-guh-TAWR-ee)

adj. powerless; futile; worthless.

✧ It's **no goo**d being a **Tory** in a Labour government.

bootless (BOOT-liss)

adj. fruitless; unprofitable; futile; useless. (ult. from the Old English *bot*, for profit).

✧ "If it's bootless, it's fr**uitless**."

274. Palladian (puh-LAY-dee-un)

adj. pertaining to wisdom and study (after Athena, the Greek goddess of wisdom, who became known as Pallas Athena after slaying a giant named Pallas and using his skin as a shield).

Palladian

adj. pertaining to the architectural style of Andreas Palladio, an Italian Renaissance architect who tried to recreate the style and proportions of ancient Rome, and whose style was revived in mid-eighteenth-century Britain.

275. **supererogatory** (soo-pur-ih-ROG-uh-tawr-ee)

adj. above and beyond the call of duty; more than is needed or required; superfluous (from the Latin *supererogare*, "to spend over and above").

✧ "The **superhero**'s supererogatory attempts to save the day were superfluous."

276. **condign** (kun-DĪN)

adj. deserving; fitting; appropriate.

277. **infandous** (in-FAN-duss)

adj. unmentionably terrible.

278. **seity** (SEE-ih-tee)

n. personality; individuality.

✧ "**See**, **it**'s all about m**e**."

279. **cacoepy** (ka-KŌ-ih-pee)

n. poor or incorrect pronunciation.

cacography (ka-KOG-ruh-fee)

n. poor handwriting.

280. **loxotic** (lok-SOT-ik)

adj. oblique; distorted.

✧ Loxotic means **lo**psided.

281. **parallax** (PAR-uh-LAKS)

n. the appearance of a difference in an object's position based on a change in the position of the observer (e.g., a star that appears to change its position relative to other stars as the earth orbits the sun; ult. from the Greek *parallassein*, to alter).

282. **solipsism** (SOL-ip-SIZ-um)

n. the belief that only the self is real and knowable (from the Latin *solus ipse*, "sole self"; George

Berkeley, an eighteenth-century philosopher, was a famous solipsist. The poet William Butler Yeats wrote of him: "And God-appointed Berkeley that proved all things a dream,/That this pragmatical, preposterous pig of a world, its farrow that so solid seem,/Must vanish in an instant if the mind but change its theme.")

✧ **Solo**-psism.

solecism (SOL-ih-SIZ-um)

n. a violation of rules or conventions, esp. an error of grammar or idiom, or a breach in manners or propriety.

✧ To confuse the word solecism with **soli**p**sism** would be a solecism.

283. doxastic (dok-SASS-tik)

adj. pertaining to opinion (orthodox has the same Greek root and literally means "upright opinion").

284. sedulous (SEJ-ul-uss)

adj. diligent; busy; industrious.

✧ Sedulous first, **sed**entary later.

285. pica (PĪ-kuh)

n. a unit of type size equal to ⅙ inch or 12 points (believed to be from the Medieval Latin for the typeface used to print a *pica*, a book of church rules, so called because of the pie eaten at church feasts; *pica* is Latin for magpie).

pica

n. a craving for strange food, as in pregnancy (in reference to the magpie's omnivorous appetite).

286. empennage (OM-peh-nozh)

n. the tail of an aircraft (from the French for feathering).

287. **pileated** (PĪL-ee-Ā-tid)

adj. crested like a mushroom or woodpecker.

✧ A woman with a hat **pile**d **at**op her **head** is pileated.

288. **hamate** (HAY-māt)

adj. hook-shaped (ult. from the Latin *hamus*, for hook).

✧ " '**Hey**, **mate**,' said Captain Hook."

falcate (FAL-kāt)

adj. sickle-shaped; curved and tapering to a point.

289. **hyetal** (HĪ-it-uhl)

adj. rainy.

estival (ESS-tih-vul)

adj. summery.

vernal (VURN-ull)

adj. springlike.

brumal (BROOM-ull)

adj. wintry.

✧ "Sweep the snow with a **broom all** away."

290. **effluvium** (ih-FLOO-vee-um)

> *n.* an outflow or rising vapor, esp. a foul-smelling one.

> ✧ Effluvium is an **i**cky out**flow**.

291. **anacreontic** (AN-uh-kree-ON-tik)

> *adj.* amatory; convivial (as in the love poems of Anacreon, a Greek poet).

> ## Pindaric (pin-DAR-ik)

> *adj.* irregular, passionate and relatively unrestrained (like the odes of the Greek poet Pindar).

292. **orrery** (AWR-ur-ee)

> *n.* a miniature planetarium; a mechanical model of the solar system (after the Earl of Orrery, the patron of the model's inventor).

293. **recreant** (REK-ree-unt)

> *adj.* cowardly or disloyal. *n.* a cowardly or disloyal person.

> ✧ One who **wreck**s **cree**ds is a recreant and a miscreant.

294. **divers** (DĪ-vurz)

> *adj.* various and sundry (diverse is a paronym [see 8] of divers).

295. **purlieu** (pur-LYOO)

> *n.* neighborhood; suburb (from the Old French *poraler*, to traverse).

> ## milieu (mil-YOO)

> *n.* environment; surroundings (from the Old French for middle place; milieu refers more to social climate, purlieu more to place).

296. emetic (ih-MEH-tik)

n. that which induces vomiting.   *adj.* vomit-inducing.

emesis (ih-MEE-siss)

n. vomiting.

297. apatetic (AP-uh-TET-ik)

adj. camouflaging; having protective imitative coloration or shape.

✧ **A pat**tern that **trick**s the eye is apatetic.

298. turbinate (TUR-bin-āt)

adj. spiraled or cone-shaped, like a shell. *v.t.* to spin; whirl (from the Latin *turbo*, a spinning top).

✧ **Turb**o-top.

299. roric (RAWR-ik)

adj. dewy (from the Latin *ros*, *roris* for dew).

300. thersitical (thur-SIT-ih-kul)

adj. loudmouthed; foulmouthed; scurrilous (after Thersites, a man who, according to Greek legend, was violent and scurrilous in speech).

✧ Thersites had a **thirs**t for cursing.

clamant (KLAY-munt)

adj. loud, insistent.

✧ A **clam**or is clamant.

301. satori (suh-TAWR-ee)

n. a sudden experience of enlightenment, usu. reached when pondering an unsolvable riddle.

302. ungual (UNG-gwul)

adj. resembling a fingernail, hoof or claw.

303. recusant (rih-KYOO-zunt)

n. a dissenter or nonconformist (refers in particular to Catholics who refused to attend Anglican Church services during the reign of Henry VIII). *adj.* disobedient; nonconformist.

✧ A recusant **refus**es.

304. autarchy, **autarky** (AW-tawr-kee)

n. 1. absolute sovereignty; despotism (literally, "self-rule"). 2. self-sufficiency, esp. in spiritual or economic matters.

✧ Noah's **ark** was an autarchy.

305. derogate (DER-uh-GĀT)

v.t., v.i. to reduce the value of; detract from.

✧ The Water**gate** scandal served to derogate the government.

306. effable (EF-uh-bul)

adj. expressible.

307. fodient (FŌ-dee-int)

adj. pertaining to digging.

308. redact (rih-DAKT)

v.t. 1. to prepare for publication; edit or revise. 2. to draw up, as in a proclamation.

✧ An editor **react**s by redacting with a red pencil.

dele (DEE-lee)

n. the proofreading mark resembling a lowercase script e, indicating that something is to be deleted.

309. satrap (SAY-trap; SAT-rap)

n. a provincial tyrant (in ancient times, a petty ruler of Persia).

✧ A satrap would use **a strap**.

310. jounce (JOUNSS)

v.i. to jolt and bounce.

311. inquiline (IN-kwih-LĪN)

adj. living in another's nest. *n.* an animal that cohabits with an animal of a different species in that animal's burrow or nest.

pensile (PEN-sīl)

adj. 1. hanging; suspended. 2. having or building a hanging nest.

312. stochastic (stō-KASS-tik)

adj. randomly determined; unpredictable; conjectural.

✧ The **stock** market is stochastic.

313. incommensurable (in-kum-MEN-sur-uh-bull)

adj. lacking a common measure or common quality upon which to make a comparison. (Some would say apples and oranges are incommensurable.)

commensal (kuh-MEN-sul)

adj. living and feeding together. *n.* such organisms or individuals (from the Latin *com* + *mensa*, literally, "together [at the] table").

314. furbish (FUR-bish)

v.t. to brighten; polish.

315. involute (IN-vuh-LOOT)

adj. intricate; complex, as in a maze.

316. tiffany (TIF-uh-nee)

n. 1. light, gauzy material; a garment made of such. 2. something insubstantial or flimsy. *adj.* light and diaphanous. (This word is far older than Charles L. Tiffany, the founder of the New York jewelers and father of the famous glassmaker Louis Comfort Tiffany. The word is derived from theophany.)

theophany (thee-AH-fuh-nee)

n. a visible manifestation of God; God in human form (from the Greek *theo*, "god," + *phainein*, "to show").

317. **metonymy** (mih-TAHN-uh-mee)

n. use of an attribute or commonly associated feature of something to denote it. (Referring to the nation's Capitol building as "the Hill" is metonymy.)

✧ Naming a cat Mittens because it appears to be wearing them is "**mitten-name-y**."

synecdoche (sin-EK-duh-kee)

n. use of a part to signify a whole (as in "all hands on deck"); or, conversely, use of a whole to signify a part (referring to a police officer as "the law").

✧ Saying "**sa**v**i**ng your **nec**k" to mean "saving your life" is synecdoche.

318. **bruit** (BROOT)

v.t. to spread around; gossip. *n.* a rumor or clamor.

✧ A bruit can be **brut**al.

319. **mulierose** (MOO-lee-ur-ōss)

adj. excessively fond of women.

✧ **Molière wro**te *Don Juan*, a play about the legendary mulierose nobleman.

320. **jussive** (JUSS-iv)

n. a word or expression that signifies command. *adj.* signifying command.

✧ "**Jus**t Do **I**t," the Nike slogan, is jussive.

321. **réclame** (ray-KLAHM)

n. public acclaim; publicity.

322. **grobian** (GRŌ-bee-un)

n. a rude or boorish person.

✧ "He could **grow** to **be** a grobian if he continues to be **in**sulting."

323. **saturnalia** (sat-ur-NĀL-yuh)

n. an unrestrained celebration; orgy (after the ancient Roman festival of Saturn).

saturnian (sa-TUR-nee-un)

adj. 1. prosperous; peaceful (after the reign of the Roman god Saturn). 2. pertaining to the planet Saturn.

saturnine (SAT-ur-nīn)

adj. 1. sad; sullen; sarcastic. 2. leaden (alchemists considered lead to be cold, like the planet Saturn).

324. claque (KLAK)

n. a group of paid applauders; a member of such.

✧ Claquers **cla**p.

325. saurian (SAWR-ee-un)

n. a lizard; the suborder of reptiles that includes lizards. *adj.* lizard-like; pertaining to lizards.

✧ Dino**saur**s were once classified as saurians.

326. lalochezia (lah-lō-KEE-zee-uh)

n. the use of lascivious language to relieve tension.

327. rictus (RIK-tuss)

n. a gaping grimace; the expanse of an open mouth (literally, "mouth opened wide" in Latin, as in Edvard Munch's painting, *The Scream*).

328. cyprian (SIP-ree-un)

adj. lecherous; wanton. (In ancient times, Aphrodite, the goddess of love, was worshiped on the island of Cyprus.)

cupreous (KOO-pree-us; KYOO-pree-us)

adj. coppery (the same Greek root as cyprian; the island of Cyprus is rich in copper).

329. renable (REN-uh-bull)

adj. eloquent; fluent; speaking or reading clearly and distinctly.

✧ "Renata's renable speech **ran** smoothly."

330. stomatic (stō-MAT-ik)

adj. pertaining to the mouth (*stoma* means mouth in Greek).

331. **adonize** (AD-un-īz)

v.t., v.i. to adorn or dandify using tattoos, piercing, makeup, etc. (after the mythical Adonis, a young mortal dandy who was the object of the Greek goddess Aphrodite's affection).

332. **conger** (KONG-gur)

n. a large, scaleless marine eel of the Congridae family.

congeries (kun-JEER-eez; KON-jur-eez)

n. a conglomeration; heap or mess.

333. **bewray**, **beray** (bih-RĀ)

v.t. to betray; reveal (a secret) prejudicially.

✧ To bewray information is to **be**t**ray** a secret, often with the intent of blaming.

deray (dih-RAY)

n. disorder; disturbance; confusion; disorderly merriment.

✧ Where there's deray, things are in **di**sar**ray**.

334. **asteism** (ASS-tee-IZ-um)

n. urbane irony; polite mockery.

charientism (KAR-ee-un-TIZ-um)

n. an elegantly veiled insult.

✧ To **carry** an **in**sult within a compliment is charientism.

335. **eristic** (eh-RISS-tik)

adj. aiming at victory rather than truth. *n.* a person given to disputation (Eris is the spirit of strife in Greek mythology; wherever Eris's golden apple of discord was thrown, quarrels broke out).

336. **cruse** (CROOZ)

n. a small earthenware pot (from the Middle English *crouse*; cruse occasionally appears in the King James Bible to denote a container for holding water, oil, honey, salt, etc.).

337. **indaba** (in-DAH-bah)

n. 1. a conference; discussion.   2. a person's business, problem or concern (originally a Zulu word for conference).

✧ "We can get together for an indaba **in the bar**."

338. **fatiferous** (fa-TIF-ur-us)

adj. deadly; destructive (literally, "fate-carrying" in Latin).

✧ **Fat**, **if for us**, is fatiferous.

339. **reify** (REE-ih-fī)

v.t. to make concrete or real.

✧ **Real**-ify.

340. **micturition** (mik-tyer-ISH-un)

n. the need for frequent urination.

✧ **Much-urination**.

diaphoresis (DĪ-uh-for-EE-siss)

n. excessive or copious sweating.

recrement (REK-rih-ment)

n. any bodily fluid.

341. **xenial** (ZEE-nee-ul)

adj. pertaining to hospitality (from the Greek *xenos*, for strange or foreign).

✧ A **xe**nophobe is neither xenial nor conge**nial**.

342. **apophasis** (uh-PAH-fuh-siss)

n. mentioning something by saying it won't be mentioned or by denying it.

343. **ectopia** (ek-TŌ-pee-uh)

n. abnormal position of an organ or part.

344. **chautauqua** (shuh-TAW-kwuh)

n. a summer school or similar educational course for adults (after a summer educational program on Chautauqua Lake in New York State that spawned a movement at the turn of the twentieth century. In its heyday, over 400 chautauquas sprang up across the country. The lake's name is believed to be a contraction of a local Native American word meaning "where the fish was taken out").

✧ "They **show** and **talk** at the chautauqua."

345. **hamartia** (HAH-mar-TEE-uh)

n. a fatal flaw (from the Greek *hamartanein*, to miss the mark or err).

hamartiology (HAH-mahr-tee-OL-uh-jee)

n. the study or doctrine of sin.

346. **amyous** (ĀM-ee-uss)

adj. weak; lacking muscle (from the Greek, literally, "not muscled").

347. **rabato** (rah-BAH-tō)

n. a standup collar (popular in the sixteenth and seventeenth centuries, as seen in many paintings of England's Elizabeth I).

rebozo (reh-BŌ-zō)

n. a mantilla-like veil or head scarf worn chiefly by Mexican women (from the Spanish *rebosar*, to muffle).

348. **colubrine** (KOL-uh-brīn)

adj. snake-like.

columbine (KOL-um-bīn)

adj. dove-like. *n.* a northern flower with honey-secreting, beaklike spurs.

349. **revanchist** (rih-VAHN-chist)

n. 1. a person out for revenge. 2. a person who seeks the return of a nation's lost territory.

350. **virtu** (vur-TOO; VUR-too)

n. 1. a work of art. 2. love of objects of art; expertise in the fine arts. 3. artistic value. 4. inherent moral worth or virtue.

351. elench (ee-LENGK), **elenchs**

n., n.pl. 1. a refutation. 2. a fallacious argument that seems true.

352. labile (LAY-bil; LAY-bull)

adj. unstable; liable to err or change.

✧ That which is labile is **l**iable to be unst**able**.

fixity (FIK-sit-ee)

n. stability; permanence.

353. patulous (PACH-uh-luss)

adj. 1. wide open; gaping. 2. spreading (of tree boughs).

354. *berceuse* (behr-SOOZ)

n. a lullaby; gently rocking instrumental piece (ult. from the French *bercer*, to rock).

355. frottage (fraw-TAHZH)

n. 1. rubbing against a clothed person in a crowd for sexual gratification. 2. the technique of taking a rubbing from an uneven surface such as grained wood to make an artistic work.

frotteur (frah-TUR)

n. one who engages in frottage.

✧ A crowded subway car could be **fraught** with frotteurs.

356. hereism (HEER-ee-iz-um)

n. faithfulness in marriage.

✧ "**Here he is, m**y faithful husband."

apistia (ap-ISS-tee-uh)

n. faithlessness in marriage.

✧ A cuckolded spouse is often **a pissed**-off one.

357. **preciosity** (PRESH-ee-AH-sih-tee)

   n. excessive elegance, esp. of literary style.

   ◇ Overly **precious** language can result
   in preciosity.

   euphuism (YOO-foo-iz-um)

   n. an affected elegance of literary style using
   heavy alliteration, elaborate similes and other
   rhetorical devices (after the fictional Euphues,
   the protagonist of works by the Elizabethan
   author John Lyly; *euphues* means shapely or
   clever in Greek).

   ◇ "**You** too can use euphuism like Euphues, by
   alliterating liberally."

358. **apical** (AP-ik-ul)

   adj. 1. articulated with the tip of the tongue
   (e.g., the consonants d and t) or pertaining to
   such. 2. pertaining to an apex.

   uvular (YOO-vyuh-lur)

   adj. 1. articulated with the back of the tongue
   against the uvula, the fleshy appendage at the
   back of the soft palate (e.g., the French r).
   2. pertaining to the uvula.

359. **obscurant** (ob-SKYUR-unt)

   n. a philistine; one who strives to prevent
   enlightenment and political reform. *adj.* 1.
   characterized by opposition to enlightenment
   and political reform. 2. tending to make
   obscure, esp. visually (as in obscurant clouds).

   obscurantist (ob-SKYUR-un-tist)

   n. a person who is deliberately vague, esp. in an
   artistic or literary work.

360. **Procrustean** (prō-KRUSS-tee-un)

adj. causing cruel and arbitrary conformity; fitting something to a preconceived idea or system (after Procrustes, a robber who, according to Greek legend, stretched or mutilated his victims to fit the length of his bed).

361. **gibbous** (GIB-uss)

adj. 1. humped; humpbacked; convex in shape. 2. pertaining to a moon that is more than half full.

362. **hylic** (HĪ-lik)

adj. pertaining to matter; material (from the Greek *hyle*, Aristotle's term for matter).

363. **claudicant** (KLAW-dik-unt)

adj. lame; limping.

✧ "**Claudi**e **can't** walk without limping."

claudent (KLAW-dent)

adj. closing; drawing together.

364. **novercal** (nō-VUR-kul)

adj. involving a stepmother (ult. from the Latin *noverca*, for stepmother).

novercal

adj. occurring every ninth year (from the Latin *novennis*, "of nine years").

365. **desinence** (DEH-sih-nenss)

n. termination; ending.

The end

Bibliography

Print Resources

Adler, Mortimer, and Robert Hutchins, eds. *Great Books of the Western World*. 54 vols. Chicago: Encyclopædia Britannica, 1952.

American Heritage Dictionary: Second College Edition. Boston: Houghton Mifflin, 1982.

Armstrong, Karen. *A History of God: The 4,000-Year Quest of Judaism, Christianity and Islam*. New York: Ballantine Books, 1993.

Ayto, John. *The Dictionary of Difficult Words*. Rev. ed. New York: Barnes & Noble, 1998.

Biard, J. D., H. Ferrar, and J. A. Hutchinson. *The Concise Oxford French Dictionary: Second Edition*. Oxford: Clarendon Press, 1984.

Bowler, Peter. *The Superior Person's Book of Words*. Boston: David R. Godine, 1985.

Brown, Lesley, ed. *The New Shorter Oxford English Dictionary: The New Authority on the English Language*. 2 vols. Oxford: Clarendon Press, 1993.

Bryson, Bill. *The Mother Tongue: English & How It Got That Way*. New York: William Morrow, 1990.

Buchanan-Brown, John, et al., eds. *Le Mot Juste: A Dictionary of Classical & Foreign Words & Phrases*. New York: Vintage, 1991.

Bulfinch, Thomas. *Bulfinch's Mythology*. New York: Modern Library, 1993.

Calasibetta, Charlotte Mankey. *Fairchild's Dictionary of Fashion*. 2 rev. ed. New York: Fairchild Books, 1998.

Castiglione, Baldessar. *The Book of the Courtier*. Trans. Sir Thomas Hoby. London, 1561.

Bibliography

Chapman, Robert L., ed. *Roget's International Thesaurus: Fourth Edition.* New York: HarperCollins, 1977.

Cmiel, Kenneth, and Ken Cmiel. *Democratic Eloquence: The Fight for Popular Speech in Nineteenth-Century America.* New York: William Morrow, 1990.

Crystal, David. *The Cambridge Encyclopedia of the English Language.* Cambridge: Cambridge University Press, 1997.

D'Aulaire, Ingrid, and Edgar Parin. *D'Aulaire's Book of Greek Myths.* Garden City, N.Y.: Doubleday, 1962.

Dickson, Paul. *Words: A Connoisseur's Collection of Old and New, Weird and Wonderful, Useful and Outlandish Words.* New York: Delacorte Press, 1982.

Elster, Charles Harrington. *There's a Word for It! A Grandiloquent Guide to Life.* New York: Pocket Books, 1997.

Farb, Peter. *Word Play: What Happens When People Talk.* New York: Vintage, 1993.

Fisher, David, and Reginald Bragonier Jr. *What's What: A Visual Glossary of the Physical World.* Maplewood, N.J.: Hammond, 1981.

Funk, Charles Earle. *2,107 Curious Word Origins, Sayings, & Expressions.* New York: Galahad Books, 1986.

Gifis, Steven H. *Law Dictionary.* Woodbury, N.Y.: Barron's Educational Series, 1975.

Glazier, Stephen. *Random House Word Menu.* New York: Random House, 1992.

Godin, Seth, and Margery Mandell. *Million Dollar Words: More than 1,000 Words to Make You Sound like a Million Bucks.* Philadelphia: Running Press, 1993.

Greenman, Robert. *Words That Make a Difference and How to Use Them in a Masterly Way.* Delray Beach, Fla.: Levenger Press, 2000.

Bibliography

Guralnik, David, ed. *Webster's New World Dictionary of the English Language: Second College Edition.* New York: Simon & Schuster, 1980.

Haubrich, William S. "Menckenisms." *Verbatim: the Language Quarterly* 24 (Autumn 1999): 20-26.

Heifetz, Josefa. *Mrs. Byrne's Dictionary of Unusual, Obscure, and Preposterous Words.* Secaucus, N.J.: University Books, 1974.

Hill, Robert H. *Jarrold's Dictionary of Difficult Words.* New York: Howell, Soskin, 1946.

Johnson, Samuel. *Samuel Johnson's Dictionary: Selections from the 1755 Work That Defined the English Language.* Ed. Jack Lynch. Delray Beach, Fla.: Levenger Press, 2002.

Lederer, Richard. *Get Thee to a Punnery!* Charleston, S.C.: Wyrick, 1988.

———. *The Miracle of Language.* New York: Pocket Books, 1991.

Liddell, H. G., and Robert Scott, eds. *An Intermediate Greek-English Lexicon.* Oxford: Clarendon Press, 1987.

Lucie-Smith, Edward. *The Thames & Hudson Dictionary of Art Terms.* London: Thames & Hudson, 1984.

McCrum, Robert. *The Story of English.* Contributions by William Cran and Robert MacNeil. New York: Viking Press, 1988.

Mencken, H. L. *The American Language.* 4th ed. New York: Alfred A. Knopf, 1949.

———. *The American Language: Supplements I and II.* New York: Alfred A. Knopf, 1952.

Middleton, A. E. "The History of Mnemonics." In *All About Mnemonics.* London, 1885.

Bibliography

Norback, Craig, and Peter Norback. *Merit Presents the "Must" Words: A Collection of 6,000 Essential Words to Help You Enrich Your Vocabulary.* N.p.: Merit, 1979.

Nurnberg, Maxwell. *I Always Look Up the Word "Egregious": A Vocabulary Book for People Who Don't Need One.* New York: Barnes & Noble, 1998.

Orwell, George. *Shooting an Elephant and Other Essays.* Reprint ed. Orlando, Fla.: Harcourt Brace, 1984.

Palmer, R. R., and Joel Colton. *A History of the Modern World.* 8th ed. New York: Alfred A. Knopf, 1995.

Quine, W. V. *Quiddities: An Intermittently Philosophical Dictionary.* Reprint. Cambridge, Mass.: Harvard University Press, 1989.

Random House College Dictionary. Rev. ed. New York: Random House, 1975.

Rheingold, Howard. *They Have a Word for It.* Los Angeles: Jeremy P. Tarcher, 1988.

Safire, William. *On Language.* New York: Avon Books, 1980.

Schur, Norman. *2000 Most Challenging and Obscure Words.* New York: Galahad Books, 1994.

Simpson, D. P. *Cassell's Latin Dictionary, First Macmillan Edition.* London: Cassell & Company, 1977.

Thomas, Lewis. *Et Cetera, Et Cetera: Notes of a Word-Watcher.* New York: Penguin Books, 1991.

Trinity Broadcasting Network Special Edition Hebrew-Greek Study Bible. Dallas: Heritage Printers & Publishers, 1984.

Verdi, John. "How We Do Things with Words: An Introduction to Wittgenstein." *St. John's Review* 44 (1998): 29–71.

Bibliography

Voltaire. *Voltaire's Philosophical Dictionary.* New York: Carlton House, n.d.

Watkins, Calvert. *The American Heritage Dictionary of Indo-European Roots.* Boston: Houghton Mifflin, 1985.

Webster's Dictionary of Synonyms: First Edition. Springfield, Mass.: G. & C. Merriam, 1942.

Webster's New International Dictionary of the English Language. 2d ed. unabridged. Springfield, Mass.: G. & C. Merriam, 1959.

Weekley, Ernest. *An Etymological Dictionary of English.* 2 vols. New York: Dover, 1967.

Internet Resources

Dates refer to the authors' most recent access before the book's publication.

Academic Search Premier. Ebsco Host Research Databases. 20 September 2002 <http://www.epnet.com/academic/acasearchprem.asp>.

The American Heritage Dictionary of the English Language: Fourth Edition. Houghton Mifflin. 16 May 2001 <http://www.eref-trade.hmco.com>.

Bartleby.com: Great Books Online. Ed. Steven H. van Leeuwen.20 September 2002 <http://www.bartleby.com>.

Beliefnet. Ed. Steven Waldman. 20 September 2002 <http://www.beliefnet.com>.

Chrisomalis, Steven. *Forthright's Phrontistery: International House of Logorrhea, The Word List.* 22 April 2002 <http://phrontistery.50megs.com>.

The Columbia Electronic Encyclopedia. Columbia University Press. Family Education Network. 20 September 2002 <http://www.infoplease.com/encyclopedia.html>.

Bibliography

Crane, Gregory R., ed. *The Perseus Project*. Dept.
    of Classics, Tufts University. 20 September 2002
    <http://www.perseus.tufts.edu>.

Dictionary.com/Word of the Day. Lexico LLC.
    20 September 2002 <http://www.dictionary.com/
    wordoftheday/archive>.

Easton's 1897 Bible Dictionary. Pub. Thomas Nelson.
    20 September 2002 <ftp://ccel.wheaton.edu/ebooks/
    HTML/e/easton/ebd>.

eLibrary. Alacritude, LLC. 30 August 2000 <http://
    www.elibrary.com>.

*Encarta World English Dictionary, North American
    Edition*. Microsoft. 20 September 2002
    <http://encarta.msn.com>.

Garg, Anu, ed. *A.Word.A.Day*. 20 September 2002
    <http://wordsmith.org/awad/archives.html>.

Hodgkin, Adam, ed. *Xrefer*. 20 September 2002
    <http://www.xrefer.com>.

Merriam-Webster Online. Merriam-Webster.
    20 September 2002 <http://www.m-w.com>.

OED Online. Ed. John Simpson. Oxford University
    Press. 9 September 2002 <http://www.oed.com>.

On-line Medical Dictionary. Academic Medical
    Publishing & CancerWEB. 29 March 2002
    <http://cancerweb.ncl.ac.ukz>.

"The Origin of New York State's County Names."
    Kids' Room: New York State Facts. New York State
    Department of State Web site. 20 September 2002
    <http://www.dos.state.ny.us/kidsroom/nysfacts/
    counties.html>.

Ross, David. "English Architecture: A History." Britain
    Express. 20 September 2002
    <http://www.britainexpress.com/architecture>.

Bibliography

Stoddard, Samuel. *Fun with Words: A Celebration of the English Language.* A Rinkworks production. 20 September 2002 <http://www.rinkworks.com/words>.

Taylor, Alan. *Luciferous Logolepsy: Dragging Obscure Words into the Light of Day.* 20 September 2002 <http://www.kokogiak.com/logolepsy>.

Webster's Revised Unabridged Dictionary [1913]. Micra. 20 September 2002 <ftp://ftp.uga.edu/pub/misc/webster>.

Weisstein, Eric. *Eric Weisstein's World of Mathematics (MathWorld).* Wolfram Web Resource. 9 September 2002 <http://mathworld.wolfram.com>.

Williams, William A. Jr., ed. *Concordances of Great Books.* 20 September 2002 <http://www.concordance.com>.

WordNet 1.6. Princeton University. 20 September 2002 <ftp://clarity.princeton.edu/pub/wordnet/wn1.6unix.tar.gz>.

Acknowledgments

If it weren't for Benjamin Lapkin and Michael Horenstein, this book would never have gone over the transom. We are grateful to Steve and Lori Leveen of Levenger for providing lamps for our lucubrations (via their catalog), and for accepting our manuscript. Special thanks to our editor, Mim Harrison, for nurturing a palmary press within Levenger, and for her care and careful redactions. We doff our hats to Lee Passarella for her lovely limning; Danielle Furci for her Tempean design; Jeff Simon, Tina St. Pierre and Megan Gordon for poring over the picas; and Dawn Hyden, Dee Moustakas and Vicki Ehrenman for their watchful eyes. We're also grateful to Peggy Montgomery, Sue Steffey and Melissa Parrott for their support and enthusiasm.

Within hours of our posting a query to the St. John's College message board for a peer reviewer, Mary Suzanne Rodriguez put us in touch with Dr. James Girsch, scholar of Medieval Latin, former associate editor of the *Middle English Dictionary*, etymology review editor for the *Encarta World English Dictionary* and senior editor of the *Thorndike Barnhart Dictionary Series*. We are indebted to Jaimie for his generous lexicographical guidance.

David Pierce, mathematician and philosopher, was as persnickety as we wanted him to be. Ditto Steve Thomas, who lent his formidable Greek expertise. Many thanks also to everyone on the J-list—in particular, Catherine Barrier, Dianne Cowan, Susan Eversole, Bill Fant, Alex Kambouris Alberstadt, Joy Kaplan, Howard Meister and Lutron the classics scholar, yclept Luis Alejandro Salas. On the johnnyXpress, thanks to Dixie Davis, Sapna Gandhi, Owen Goldin, Nick Irsfeld, Craig LeFevre and Edith Updike. The novelist William Kowalski sent writerly encouragement and advice from somewhere north of here, and we are humbled and grateful.

At Cambridge University Press, thanks to Jae Hong, Marc Anderson and Ted Gerney. We are also much

Acknowledgments

obliged to Doug Hernandez and Christine Smith at Harcourt, and to Diane Beaver at the Seneca Nation of Indians Library. We send kudos to Nancy Branscome Murphy, Annette Hunt, Tracy Kerievsky and Jerry Wexler.

Finally, we would like to give special recognition to three special people: Young Ja Kim, Wendie Myles and Lynda Myles (Hallie's mother), for their macarism and encouragement.

Index of Words

Numbers refer to page numbers.

Index of Words

C

cacoepy, 68
cacography, 68
caducity, 43
canaille, 58
cantillate, 33
caparison, 30
captation, 44
captious, 44
casuistry, 35
catabasis, 27
catachresis, 33
catadromous, 23
causerie, 63
cecity, 47
cervine, 56
cervisial, 56
Chaldean, 67
charientism, 78
chautauqua, 80
chiasmus, 34
chiromancy, 67
chrestomathy, 64
clamant, 72
claque, 77
claudent, 84
claudicant, 84
clavate, 52
clinquant, 39
colletic, 17
colubrine, 81
columbine, 81
commensal, 74
concinnity, 20
condign, 68
congener, 26
conger, 78
congeries, 78
consuetude, 41

contronym, 29
corrigendum, 63
coruscate, 18
costive, 56
cozen, 37
crepitate, 67
crepuscular, 66
cruse, 79
cunctation, 38
cupreous, 77
cursorial, 20
cyprian, 77

D

Daphnean, 32
dele, 73
deliquesce, 30
Delphic, 20
demit, 65
demotic, 46
deray, 78
deric, 62
derogate, 73
desinence, 84
detrition, 20
detritus, 20
diapason, 52
diaphoresis, 80
dimication, 27
Dionysian, 39
distal, 26
divers, 71
docity, 26
dotation, 31
doxastic, 69
drupe, 19
dulocracy, 63
dulosis, 63

Index of Words

E

F

G

Index of Words

gressorial, 20
grobian, 76
gulosity, 29

H

haha, 39
hamartia, 81
hamartiology, 81
hamate, 70
haptic, 30
hebetic, 55
hebetude, 55
Hegelian, 30
hegira, 37
hejira. *See* hegira
henotic, 22
hereism, 82
hermeneutic, 55
hermeneutical. *See*
    hermeneutic
Hesperian, 34
heuristic, 24
hirrient, 55
homunculus, 42
hyetal, 70
hylic, 84

I

illude, 58
imbue, 29
impetrate, 36
impignorate. *See*
    pignorate
impudicity, 34
inanition, 23
incommensurable, 74
incunabula, 17
indaba, 79
indict, 44

indite, 43
ineluctable, 65
infandous, 68
inficete, 54
inquiline, 74
insulse, 32
invidious, 63
involute, 74
irenic, 22

J

jongleur, 60
jounce, 74
jugal, 65
jussive, 76

K

kakistocracy, 38
kemp, 29
kleptocracy, 38
koftgari, 23

L

labile, 82
lacuna, 54
lalochezia, 77
Laodicean, 54
lenocinant, 17
lenticular, 21
ligulate, 22
limbate, 25
limn, 53
litotes, 53
littoral, 54
louche, 40
lowery, 49
loxotic, 68
lucubrate, 42
lumpen, 58

Index of Words

Index of Words

parallax, 68
parietal, 49
paronomasia, 18
paronym, 17
parure, 62
parviscient, 40
patulous, 82
pelf, 50
pendragon, 29
pensile, 74
perfervid, 66
periapt, 60
peripatetic, 21
peripeteia, 21
petrous, 45
philtrum, 57
phrontistery, 40
pica, 69
piceous, 42
pignorate, 38
pileated, 70
Pindaric, 71
pistic, 37
plutology, 27
poiesis, 31
postiche, 22
potamic, 48
pother, 49
praedial. *See* predial
preciosity, 83
preconize, 50
predial, 62
prelapsarian, 52
prescient, 40
pretermit, 34
previse, 47
pridian, 48
privative, 59
procacity, 47
procellous, 46

procerity, 42
Procrustean, 84
proem, 19
proreption, 66
prosody, 21
protean, 59
prurient, 32
pruritic, 32
purlieu, 71

Q

quiddity, 29
quietus, 50
quoddity, 29

R

rabato, 81
rabelaisian, 60
rasorial, 46
rebozo, 81
réclame, 76
recreant, 71
recrement, 80
recusant, 73
redact, 73
reify, 80
remanent, 27
remanet, 27
remeant, 27
renable, 77
revanchist, 81
revehent, 22
revenant, 22
rictus, 77
riposte, 45
risorial, 46
roborant, 60
roborean, 60
roric, 72

Index of Words

rubric, 28
rugate, 25
rutilant, 28

S

satori, 72
satrap, 73
saturnalia, 76
saturnian, 76
saturnine, 76
satyagraha, 43
saurian, 77
sciolism, 24
scopophilia, 35
scoptic, 47
scopulate, 52
scree, 57
screed, 57
secant, 47
secern, 42
sedulous, 69
seity, 68
selvage, 25
sennet, 18
sere, 51
seriatim, 66
sericeous, 51
sinciput, 57
soigné, 55
solanaceous, 19
solecism, 69
solipsism, 68
spall, 36
sprezzatura, 48
stenotic, 62
sthenic, 37
stochastic, 74
stocious, 44
stomatic, 77

strabismic, 40
suberose. *See* suberous
suberous, 45
sui generis, 25
sumpsimus, 38
supererogatory, 68
suppletion, 62
syndetic, 21
synecdoche, 75
syntomy, 35

T

talionic, 58
tantric, 22
telarian, 32
Tempean, 65
tessitura, 48
tetricity, 44
Thalian, 54
thaumatology, 55
thaumaturgic, 55
thecate, 35
theodicy, 24
theophany, 75
thersitical, 72
threnody, 63
tiffany, 74
tmesis, 44
traduce, 58
trophic, 64
turbinate, 72

U

ubiety, 62
ullage, 23
undulant, 40
ungual, 72
urticate, 64
uvular, 83

Index of Words

V

venal, 57
venery, 60
venial, 57
vernal, 70
villous, 64
virtu, 81
vulpine, 46

W

webster, 33
whilom, 38

X

xenial, 80
xeric, 22

Y

yclept, 55

Z

zarf, 26
zoetic, 26

About the Authors

Jan Leighton and Hallie Leighton are a father-and-daughter team of word collectors. Mr. Leighton grew up in a multilingual household, where he started collecting rare words when he was seven and heard his mother refer to the movie theater as *cinematograph*.

Collecting uncommon words became a lifelong pursuit. He continued collecting during his Air Force tour of Europe and North Africa (*purlieu* and *zarf*), his music studies at the University of Mexico (*berceuse*) and his classes in stage directing with Lee Strasburg (*vitiate*). He graduated from the American Theater Wing in New York City in the class with Bob Fosse (*fosse* is a rare word). A winner of more than two dozen performing awards, Mr. Leighton has portrayed more than 3,000 historical personages, including Joyce, Twain, Shakespeare, Noah Webster and others who have enriched our language with memorable words.

Hallie Leighton started collecting words at thirteen when she encountered *hussar* and *bivouac* in Tolstoy's *War and Peace*. She continued her hobby while studying drama at the High School of Performing Arts in New York City (*scrim* and *réclame*), and while reading Great Books of the Western World at St. John's College in Annapolis, Maryland, and Santa Fe, New Mexico (*peripatetic* and *arroyo*). After receiving a Bachelor of Arts in the college's classical liberal arts program, Ms. Leighton worked at Random House and in the editorial offices of Alfred A. Knopf (*pica* and *pixelate*). She has studied Hebrew, French and Latin, and continued her classical studies at Hunter College in New York, where she translated Plato's *Euthyphro*. Ms. Leighton is currently a freelance writer.

Both Leightons live in Manhattan.